The Pilgrim's Progress Study Guide

A Bible Study Based on John Bunyan's Pilgrim's Progress
Part 1

By Alan Vermilye

BROWN CHAIR BOOKS
BOOKS THAT INSPIRE

The Pilgrim's Progress Study Guide:
A Bible Study Based on John Bunyan's Pilgrim's Progress
Part 1

Copyright © 2020 Alan Vermilye
Brown Chair Books

ISBN-13: 978-1-948481-14-4

To learn more about this Bible study, to order additional copies, or to download the answer guide, visit **www.BrownChairBooks.com**.

Version 2

Table of Contents

Required Book for Study

Do you have the right book for this study?

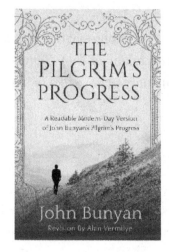

Although there are many versions of this Bunyan classic, *The Pilgrim's Progress: A Modern-Day Revised Version of John Bunyan's Pilgrims Progress* is the only book that is made specifically for this study.

Each chapter, subsection, and study question is designed to be used in conjunction with each other. Other books will feel drastically different and not match up with the study questions and format of this study.

Why is that? Well, Bunyan's original version of the book is not only very difficult to read but is broken into ten segments that he refers to as "stages" rather than the twelve chapters and subsections that this book and study utilize. Other more "readable" versions might include chapter headings, but it will not align with the sessions that correspond with this study. In addition, many leave out key text and do not keep with Bunyan's original intentions for the book.

If you are completing this study in a group setting, it would also be helpful if each participant had the same book to make class discussion time more beneficial.

Learn more about this book at www.BrownChairBooks.com.

Course Notes and Study Format

The Pilgrim's Progress Study Guide is divided into twelve weekly study sessions that correspond with the twelve chapters of *The Pilgrim's Progress: A Modern Revised Version of John Bunyan's The Pilgrim's Progress*. This study guide can be used for individual study or for weekly small groups that gather to discuss each chapter.

HOW TO USE THIS STUDY GUIDE

Each week you will read a chapter in the book and answer the questions that correspond with that chapter. The book and study have been divided up to allow plenty of time to read each chapter and answer questions in a week's time. Many of the sections are very short and will not require much time, while others are a little longer.

As you read, make notes in your book and underline or highlight sections that interest you. As you work through each session, make note of other questions or observations that you would like to share in your small group time.

GROUP FORMAT

The study is ideal for Sunday school classes as well as midweek times at the church or in the homes of group members. Session length is variable, but ideally, you should allow at least 60 minutes per session. If you feel that you cannot get through all the questions in a single session, pick and choose the questions you want to make sure you cover.

Pace yourself or your group, and do not rush the study. If you feel you need additional weeks for certain sections, be flexible and allow the learning process and class discussion to happen naturally. It's most helpful for learning purposes if each person has their own book and study guide and works through the questions prior to each class. However, couples might find it convenient to share a book.

ANSWER AND SCRIPTURE REFERENCE GUIDES

The answers to each question as well as a Scripture Reference Guide can be found at www.BrownChairBooks.com. However, do not cheat yourself. Work through each session prior to viewing the answers. The Scripture Reference Guide is a handy tool that saves time in class that would be spent looking up Bible passages.

Author Summary

John Bunyan was born in Elstow near Bedford, England, in 1628. His parents were poor, and his father was a metalworker, or "tinker," who traveled around mending pots and pans; John followed in his father's trade. He had no formal education but learned to read and write.

Although we have few details about his early life, in his autobiography, *Grace Abounding to the Chief of Sinners*, he tells us that he was not encouraged in matters of spirituality at home. He was rough, enjoyed dancing and playing tipcat, and was given to "cursing, swearing, lying and blaspheming the holy name of God."

In 1644 Bunyan lost both his mother and sister Margaret. Later that same year, when an edict demanded 225 recruits from Bedford, he entered the Parliamentary Army as a private at the age of sixteen.

There are few details about his military service, which took place during the English Civil War. However, during one battle, a fellow soldier was killed when he requested to go forward in Bunyan's place. This dramatic event led Bunyan to believe God had spared his life for some purpose. His military service exposed him to a variety of religious sects while indulging in all sorts of ungodly behavior.

Bunyan spent nearly three years in the army before returning home in 1647 to continue his trade as a metal worker. His father was now remarried and had more children, so Bunyan moved to a cottage in Elstow High Street.

His first marriage, in 1648, was to a girl who was poor like himself but came from a godly family. Her name is not known, but she owned two books, of which Bunyan said, "Her only portion was two volumes which her father had given her, 'The Plain Man's Pathway,' and 'The Practice of Piety.' In these I sometimes read, wherein I found some things pleasant to me."

During his first five years of marriage, his wife would have a profound influence on his life as he began to attend church regularly and gave up his sinful life. He also began to pore over the Scriptures, leading him to his own thoughts about conviction that he would later write about in detail.

He joined a Baptist society at Bedford and by 1653 had become a lay preacher as a member of the congregation at Bedford. Over time, Bunyan's popularity exploded, and great crowds in the thousands would come to hear him preach.

Bunyan and his wife's first child, Mary, was born blind in 1650. They would have three more children: Elizabeth, Thomas, and John. But in 1658, ten years into their marriage, Bunyan's wife died, leaving him with four small children under ten. A year later, in 1659, he got remarried to an eighteen-year-old young woman named Elizabeth.

However, their first year of marriage was interrupted when the religious tolerance that had allowed Bunyan to preach was curtailed when the monarchy was restored to power. In 1660 King Charles II came to the throne and ordered that all preachers that did not belong to the Church of England be imprisoned or banished.

Bunyan was no longer allowed to preach at the Anglican church where his congregation met. Still, he continued preaching in other places and later that year was warned that he would soon be arrested. He refused to escape and was arrested and sentenced to three months imprisonment. He was threatened with more jail time, banishment from England, and possible execution if he did not agree to stop preaching.

Although he could have his freedom whenever he wanted it, Bunyan refused to renounce preaching, opting to stand firm and keep a clear conscience instead; he was imprisoned for a total of 12 years in the Bedford County Jail.

Bunyan's imprisonment brought great hardship to his family. Elizabeth, who was pregnant at the time of his arrest, would later give birth to a stillborn child. She continually made attempts to secure her husband's release while caring for Bunyan's four small children, one of whom was blind. She relied on the charity of fellow church members and on what little Bunyan could earn in prison making shoelaces.

On occasion, he was allowed out of prison, where he attended the Bedford meetings and even preached. His daughter Sarah was born during his imprisonment, and a son, Joseph, was born after his release.

While imprisoned, he became the pastor of a congregation of inmates and stayed busy writing religious tracts, sermons, and nine books, including *Grace Abounding to the Chief of Sinners*, which was published in 1666.

In 1671 King Charles II issued a declaration of religious indulgences that released thousands of non-conformists from prison, including Bunyan in 1672.

He immediately returned to preaching but three years later was put back in jail again for around six months. It was during this time that he began work on *The Pilgrim's Progress*, which was published after his release.

Bunyan was never jailed again but spent the last 15 years of his life preaching all over England, including a visit to London every year to deliver sermons to large Baptist congregations.

In August 1688, on his way to London to preach, Bunyan went to Reading Berkshire on a ministerial visit to help resolve a quarrel between a father and son. As he returned to London on horseback, he was caught in a heavy rainstorm and fell ill with a violent fever, dying at the age of 60.

He died at the house of his friend, John Strudwick, a grocer and chandler on Snow Hill in Holborn. His grave lies in the cemetery at Bunhill Fields in London.

Book Summary

John Bunyan's *The Pilgrim's Progress* was first published in 1678 and is second only to the Bible in the number of copies sold, having never been out of print. Written almost 350 years ago, Bunyan created the most famous allegory in all of English literature while imprisoned in the Bedford County Jail.

Charles Spurgeon, known as the "Prince of Preachers," loved the book and said, "Next to the Bible, the book I value most is John Bunyan's *Pilgrim's Progress*. I believe I have read it through at least a hundred times. It is a volume of which I never seem to tire; and the secret of its freshness is that it is so largely compiled from the Scriptures."

The Pilgrim's Progress is considered one of the first novels ever written and was standard in most nineteenth century households, being read alongside the Bible. Bunyan chose an allegorical narrative to tell his powerful presentation of what it means to follow the narrow way of Christian salvation so that the lowest classes in English society would be able to understand it.

The Pilgrim's Progress is told from the narrator's perspective, as if he were in a dream. In this dream, he tells the story of Christian, a man who lives in the City of Destruction. One day Christian is awakened to the realities of sin and judgment on his life, symbolized by a heavy burden that he carries on his back. He encounters a spiritual guide named Evangelist, who sets him on the path to salvation. He must first travel to the Wicket Gate and then on to the Celestial City. Unable to convince his family and friends to travel with him, Christian sets out on his own.

Shortly after leaving, he encounters Mr. Worldly Wiseman, who leads him astray by convincing him to take an easier route that almost leads to his destruction at the Village of Morality. Once he arrives at the Wicket Gate, he is permitted entrance, setting him on his real journey on a path referred to as the Way.

Next, he arrives at the Interpreter's House, where he visits many rooms and learns lessons about his newfound faith. Once enlightened, he continues traveling to the cross and tomb, where he understands the sacrifice that Christ made for his sins; the burden rolls off his back and into the tomb. Angels arrive and provide him new clothes to wear along the Way and a certificate that he must provide for entrance to the Celestial City.

At the foot of the Hill of Difficulty, he encounters Formalism and Hypocrisy, who had climbed over the gate to get on the Way but were eventually destroyed when they would not follow the narrow path. Christian stays on the path and eventually comes upon a shady arbor, where he falls asleep, loses his scroll, and later must retrace his steps to find it.

He next arrives at the Palace Beautiful, at the top of the hill, and is admitted in by a group of four sisters. They examine his conscience and provide him with shelter and supplies for the journey, including a suit of armor.

As he travels down the hill into the Valley of Humiliation, he battles and defeats a notorious monster named Apollyon, who tries to kill him. He then proceeds through the dark and desert-like Valley of the Shadow of Death, which is haunted by demons, before catching up with his old friend, Faithful, and they exchange stories of their journey.

They are soon joined once again by Evangelist, who warns them about the wicked town of Vanity Fair, which they will soon enter. This town hosts a year-round carnival designed to tempt pilgrims to abandon their journeys. Upon arrival, they are mocked by the townspeople for their backward way of thinking and arrested under the false charge of inciting a riot. Faithful is tried, tortured, and burnt at the stake. Christian miraculously escapes and is joined by Hopeful, a recent convert from Vanity Fair, and they continue their journey together.

On the Way, they cross paths with By-ends and his friends and discuss whether it's wrong to use religion as a means to get ahead in the world. Christian and Hopeful reject By-ends and his company and enter the plain of Ease, where they are tempted by a smooth-talker named Lucre to come over and look at a silver mine. They do not succumb to temptation but pass him by.

Next they arrive at the River of God and experience some rest and relaxation. When they leave the comforts of the river, however, the road soon becomes rocky and hard, so they opt for an easier, smoother path over the fence. This bad decision leads to them getting lost and trapped in a storm and eventually captured by Giant Despair. The giant imprisons them in Doubting Castle and tortures and starves them while also encouraging them to commit suicide. Christian and Hopeful manages to escape when Christian remembers that he possesses the key of Promise, which can unlock any door in the castle.

The two pilgrims continue on their journey until they reach the Delectable Mountains, where they meet a group of shepherds and are shown a variety of wonders. The shepherds provide them a map to avoid traps along the Way and warn them to avoid the Flatterer.

Now in their final stretch to the Celestial City, they encounter a young man named Ignorance, who entered the path by a shortcut and not by the Wicket Gate. They engage in conversation with him about whether living a good life is sufficient to prove one's faith. Ignorance is unable to handle Christian's rebuke and leaves their company.

Eventually, they come to a fork in the road, and instead of reading the map the shepherds had provided, they take the wrong path and then are ensnared by Flatterer. They are rescued by an angel who punishes them for not heeding the warnings of the shepherds.

They manage to get back on the Way and then enter the Enchanted Ground, where they are warned not to fall asleep. To stay awake and alert, they discuss Hopeful's journey to becoming a Christian.

Next they encounter Atheist, who denies the Celestial City exists, claiming to have been searching for it for a long time. Christian and Hopeful avoid his trap and once again cross paths with Ignorance, whom they earnestly try to help without success as Ignorance grows frustrated and leaves again.

As Christian and Hopeful approach the land of Beulah, which borders the Celestial City, they are refreshed again for the remaining journey ahead. To reach the city, they must first cross the River of Death, which is to die. The depth of the river changes to reflect the doubt or faith of the person who enters it. At first Christian is overwhelmed by doubt and nearly drowns, but Hopeful reminds him of Christ's love. Reminded and revived, they both now have the confidence to cross over and are met by angels, who escort them the rest of the way.

At last they arrive at the gates of the Celestial City and are surrounded by a choir of angels with trumpet fanfares. They provide their certificates to the King and are transfigured as they enter the city and are welcomed by the joyous celebration of its residents.

The story ends with Ignorance arriving at the gate, but because he doesn't have a certificate to provide to the King, he is bound and taken to hell. With the pilgrim's progress to heaven now complete, the author awakes from his dream.

Character Summary

THE NARRATOR

The narrator is an anonymous person, most likely Bunyan, who is wandering in the wilderness then lays down in a clearing to sleep. He dreams the story of a pilgrim named Christian and his adventures on the Way to the Celestial City.

CHRISTIAN

Christian, once known as Graceless, is the protagonist who flees his hometown, the City of Destruction, for fear that God is going to destroy it. He carries a heavy burden on his back representing the fears for his own soul, so he leaves his family to journey to the Celestial City in search of a cure for his burden. Along the way, he meets various characters who either bring him closer to his goal or lead him off the path. Over the course of his journey, he grows in knowledge and wisdom and learns from his missteps.

EVANGELIST

Evangelist is a messenger of the gospel who serves as Christian's spiritual guide. He is eager to help Christian understand his burden and how to get rid of it. He provides instructions on beginning his journey to the Celestial City and reappears occasionally to set Christian back on the right track or provide instructions.

OBSTINATE

Obstinate is Christian's neighbor from the City of Destruction who chases after him and unsuccessfully tries to convince him to return. He dislikes change and thinks Christian is a fool for leaving the wonderful life that he has in the City of Destruction.

PLIABLE

Pliable is also Christian's neighbor from the City of Destruction and joins Obstinate in chasing after him to convince him to return home. However, after hearing more about the wonders of the Celestial City, he decides to join Christian on his pilgrimage. But his journey is short lived when he becomes frustrated after falling into the Swamp of Despair. He leaves Christian only to return home discouraged and mocked by the townspeople.

HELP

Help assists Christian by pulling him out of the Swamp of Despair and setting him back on the right path.

WORLDLY WISEMAN

Worldly Wiseman is a reasonable and practical man who is held in high esteem among those who know him. He fools Christian into believing that his burden can be removed quickly and easily by settling down in the village of Morality and following the guidance of Mr. Legality and his son.

MR. LEGALITY

Mr. Legality runs the village of Morality, along with his son, representing the Ten Commandments.

THE INTERPRETER

The Interpreter resides in a large house where pilgrims stop for instructions, for guidance, and to be become equipped in allegorical understanding. He instructs Christian by showing him a series of vignettes, each with a hidden religious meaning, and Christian eventually learns to interpret the signs himself.

ANGELS

Angels appear periodically throughout the book, acting as guardians for Christian's journey and providing him guidance, resources, and correction.

SIMPLE, LAZY, AND ARROGANCE

Simple, Lazy, and Arrogance are three men whom Christian encounters after leaving the cross who have a very naïve attitude toward the world.

FORMALISM AND HYPOCISY

Formalism and Hypocrisy are traveling companions who climb over the wall onto the Way instead of entering at the Wicket Gate. They show outward forms of religion but are void of the gospel in their hearts. They lose their lives at the foot of the Hill of Difficulty.

NERVOUSNESS AND MISTRUST

Nervousness and Mistrust are traveling companions whom Christian encounters heading to Zion, but due to the increasing danger they encounter along the Way, they become afraid and return home.

WATCHFUL

Watchful is the porter at the Palace Beautiful and is the overseer of the palace who stands guard to make sure that only genuine believers come in.

THE FOUR SISTERS OF THE PALACE BEAUTIFUL

The four sisters of the Palace Beautiful (Discretion, Prudence, Piety, and Charity) help passing pilgrims find their way on the path. They examine Christian's conscience and provide him shelter and supplies for the journey ahead, including a suit of armor.

APOLLYON

Apollyon is a notorious monster with fish scales, bear feet, dragon wings, and a lion's mouth. Christian encounters Apollyon in the Valley of Humiliation, defeating him but narrowly escaping his own death.

FAITHFUL

Faithful is a good friend of Christian's from the City of Destruction. They meet up on the Way as they both emerge from the Valley of the Shadow of Death and become traveling companions until they reach Vanity Fair. There they are mocked by the townspeople for their backward way of thinking and arrested under the false charge of inciting a riot. Faithful is tried, tortured, and burned at the stake and then ushered straight to Heaven.

TALKATIVE

Talkative is an attractive, bold, enthusiastic, and well-spoken man whom Christian and Faithful meet along the Way. Even though he is well versed in talking about the things of God, Christian is concerned that Talkative fails to live by what he professes.

LORD HATE-GOOD

Lord Hate-good is a cruel and unjust judge in Vanity Fair whom Christian and Faithful face for charges of disturbing the peace and dividing the town by swaying some to accept their views. He sentences Faithful to death.

HOPEFUL

Hopeful is from Vanity Fair but was persuaded to become a pilgrim after witnessing the persecution of Christian and Faithful. He joins Christian on the Way and becomes a loyal companion and good conversationalist all the way to the Celestial City. He is encouraging and sees hope in situations when Christian does not.

BY-ENDS

By-Ends is a wealthy man from the town of Fair-speech who desires money and social standing above all else and has no issue about using religion to obtain those things. He claims to follow Christ but is a hypocrite and only embraces religion for the most favorable outcome and social profit, not for personal holiness.

DEMAS

Demas runs the silver mine on the side of a hill called Lucre meaning greedy profit. He tries to persuade Christian and Hopeful to leave the Way and come to the mine for silver.

VAIN-CONFIDENCE

Vain-Confidence leads Christian and Hopeful astray after they leave the Way, opting for an easier path. He trusts in his own abilities rather than God's and meets a painful demise.

GIANT DESPAIR

Giant Despair is the master at Doubting Castle and imprisons Christian and Hopeful for trespassing on his property. He represents the temptation of despair and depression that results when we do not manage the conviction of our sin in a biblical way.

DIFFIDENCE

Diffidence is Giant Despair's wife who viciously encourages the harsh punishment of Christian and Hopeful in Doubting Castle.

THE SHEPHERDS

The Shepherds (Knowledge, Experience, and Watchful) live on the Delectable Mountains just on the edge of the Enchanted Grounds. They provide support, education, and warnings for Christian and Hopeful as they begin the last leg of their journey.

IGNORANCE

Ignorance is a very lively young man who enters the Way by a shortcut, not at the Wicket Gate. He assumes that just living a good life will provide him access to the Celestial City and places all his confidence in his own abilities rather than that of Christ. When he arrives at the gates of Heaven, he is ushered straight to Hell because he does not have the right certification.

TURN-AWAY

Turn-away is an apostate whom Christian and Hopeful observe being seized by seven devils, tied with cords, and carried to Hell. He represents those who know the truth and once made a profession of faith but have since turned away from that saving faith.

LITTLE FAITH

Little Faith unwisely lets his guard down, falls asleep in a dangerous intersection, and is robbed of his money. Although the thieves do not rob him of his jewels (his faith), he is left to beg for the remainder of his journey.

FLATTERER

Flatterer appears as a dark man wearing a white robe to conceal his real identity and induces Christian and Hopeful to follow him. He speaks with authority, showing interest and claiming he knows the way to the Celestial City but leading them into a trap instead.

ATHEIST

Atheist encounters Christian and Hopeful walking in the opposite direction of the Celestial City. He claims to have been searching for the City for over twenty years with no success and now he no longer seeks eternal life and is going home. He mocks the pilgrims for continuing their journey.

TEMPORARY

Temporary is a would-be pilgrim from Graceless. He is an unbeliever who is trying to live a moral and good life but is surrounded by those who lure him away from the faith. He ends up backsliding before his spiritual progress is complete.

Places Summary

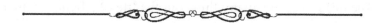

CITY OF DESTRUCTION

The City of Destruction is Christian's hometown and is a symbol of the entire world, with all its sins, corruptions, and sorrow and with no hope of salvation. He decides to flee when he learns that the city will be destroyed by the wrath of God, setting him off on his pilgrimage to the Celestial City.

SWAMP OF DESPAIR

The Swamp of Despair is the first obstacle Christian faces on his way to the Wicket Gate. Here, pilgrims are likely to become so overwhelmed with conviction over their sin that they enter a state of depression and discouragement and get bogged down and trapped in the mire.

VILLAGE OF MORALITY

The Village of Morality is run by Mr. Legality and his sons. Mr. Worldly Wiseman recommends that this is the best place for Christian to go in order to quickly rid himself of his burden as well as a wonderful place to stay and raise a family.

WICKET GATE

The Wicket Gate is the only entrance to the Way, which puts pilgrims on the narrow path to the Celestial City. The gate represents Christ, and passing through it represents one's conversion.

HOUSE OF THE INTERPRETER

The House of the Interpreter has many rooms, where Christian learns many metaphorical lessons about his new faith that spur him to religious thinking.

THE CROSS

The Cross is located on higher ground, and at the foot of it is a tomb. When Christian approaches the Cross, the burden on his back rolls off and into the tomb.

HILL OF DIFFICULTY

The Hill of Difficulty stands between Christian and the Palace Beautiful and must be climbed in order to get there. The hill represents many things in the life of a believer, including opposition, persecution, temptations, physical difficulties, overcoming sinful habits, forgiveness, etc.

PALACE BEAUTIFUL

The Palace Beautiful is at the top of the Hill of Difficulty and is where four sisters live (Discretion, Prudence, Piety, and Charity). They examine the conscience of passing pilgrims and provide them shelter and supplies for their journey, including a suit of armor.

VALLEY OF HUMILIATION

The Valley of Humiliation is located at the bottom of the Hill of Difficulty. Here, Christian is attacked by a fiendish monster named Apollyon. The Valley of Humiliation is a point in time when we throw down our pride and recognize that we are nothing without God.

VALLEY OF THE SHADOW OF DEATH

The Valley of the Shadow of Death is a darker and more fearful place than the Valley of Humiliation. Christian proceeds through the dark and desert-like valley haunted by demons and finds that his best defense is prayer. The Valley of the Shadow of Death represents the trials, temptations, and tribulations we go through in the Christian life.

VANITY FAIR

Vanity Fair is a wicked town that hosts a year-long carnival designed to tempt pilgrims to abandon their journeys. Christian and Faithful are mocked by the townspeople for their backward way of thinking and arrested under the false charge of inciting a riot. Faithful is tried, tortured, and burned at the stake.

RIVER OF GOD

The River of God is a peaceful place that's adorned with beautiful meadows full of lilies on both sides of the river and is green all year long. There are all kinds of fruit, and Christian and Hopeful eat the leaves to prevent sickness as well as to provide other medicinal benefits.

DOUBTING CASTLE

Doubting Castle is located off the narrow way that Christian and Hopeful take when they think they have found an easier path. Its master is Giant Despair, and he and his wife, Diffidence, capture, imprison, and torture the pilgrims until they manage to escape. The dungeon of Doubting Castle is a miserable, unforgiving place representing the doubts and fears of those who feel trapped under the weight of their sin.

DELECTABLE MOUNTAINS

The Delectable Mountains contain gardens, orchards, vineyards, and fountains of water. There are four shepherds who reside there (Experience, Knowledge, Watchful, and Sincere) who show Christian and Hopeful a variety of wonders, provide them with a map to avoid traps along the Way, and warn them to beware of the Flatterer.

ENCHANTED GROUND

The Enchanted Ground is a place where, if pilgrims fall asleep, they might never wake. It represents a time in our lives when things are going relatively easy and smoothly and we become spiritually complacent.

THE COUNTRY OF BEULAH

The Country of Beulah is a place of safety that borders Heaven and is within sight of the Celestial City, where angels commonly walk. It is a land of abundant provision and far beyond the reach of the temptations of this life. Christian and Hopeful stop there to rest before entering the River of Death.

THE RIVER OF DEATH

The River of Death is a deep and foreboding river that Christian and Hopeful must cross to reach the gate of the Celestial City. The depth of the river changes to reflect the doubt or faith of the person who enters it.

THE CELESTIAL CITY

The Celestial City on Mount Zion, or Heaven, is the final destination for Christian and Hopeful. Once admitted through the gate by the King, or God, they are surrounded by a choir of angels with trumpet fanfares and are welcomed by the joyous celebration of its residents.

Session 1: Chapter 1

Fleeing the City of Destruction

1. A pilgrimage is often defined as a long journey to some sacred place as an act of religious devotion. How is our spiritual life similar to that of a pilgrimage or journey? In what way does God invite us into a pilgrimage with Him in Matthew 7:7–8?

2. In his dream, Bunyan sees a poor, ragged man standing off by himself in the fields, a heavy burden on his back and a book in his hand. According to Isaiah 64:6, what do the rags the man is wearing represent in this story?

3. Read Psalm 38:4. What does the heavy burden the man is carrying represent?

4. What book is the man carrying, and what happens to him after reading it? Read Hebrews 4:12 and Romans 3:19–20. How would you describe the piercing power of God's Word?

5. The man tells his family and friends of the coming destruction and the need to flee immediately. At first, they treat him as though he's sick or perhaps mentally ill. Eventually they become angry with him, mock him, and ignore him. Why do some people respond not only with indifference but with outright antagonism toward those seeking God? How should we respond to those that try to dampen our spiritual interest?

6. One day as he's walking alone, reading his book, he's overcome with his spiritual burden and begins to cry aloud. A man named Evangelist approaches him to see what is wrong. Who does Evangelist represent? What two reasons does the man give for being unwilling to die?

7. Evangelist advised him to "flee from the wrath to come." Match the following verses with the correct allegorical representations found in the story.

___ Wicket Gate   a. Psalm 119:105

___ The Light   b. Matthew 7:7–8

___ Knock on the Gate   c. Matthew 7:13–14

8. Do you think many people come to God today out of conviction or simply in hopes of having their problems solved?

In Pursuit of Christian

1. Why do you think Bunyan describes Christian's world as "The City of Destruction?" Do you think that's an accurate description of our world today? Why or why not?

2. The word obstinate means to stubbornly refuse to change your opinion despite being persuaded. How would you describe Christian's neighbor Obstinate? According to Jeremiah 6:10, who would he represent?

3. Review the arguments Obstinate uses to discourage Christian below. Which do you think would have been the most difficult for you to hear if you were Christian?

    A. Reminding you of everything you're giving up
    B. Speaking sarcastically and belittling God's Word
    C. Being talked down to and called names
    D. Questioning your judgment or intellect for following Christ

4. The word pliable means easily bent or flexible. How would you describe Christian's neighbor Pliable, and who would he represent? Pliable has no burden on his back yet still follows Christian. Why?

5. Read Luke 9:62. What does Christian mean when he says he can't go back because "he put his hand on the plow"? What is the danger in looking back to our previous life?

A Conversation with Pliable

1. Pliable is not complaining about a burden on his back nor does he show any interest in his sin or forgiveness. What seemed to be his main concern regarding the glories of heaven?

2. Do you think Christian's desire for company on his journey overshadowed his judgment regarding Pliable's true motives for joining him?

Battling the Swamp of Despair

1. Why did Pliable turn back and go home after he was so excited to start on the journey? How did he get out of the swamp so much easier than Christian?

2. How is Pliable like the "hearer" that Jesus illustrates in the parable of the sower in Matthew 13:20–21?

3. Have you ever known someone who started off so excited to follow Christ but then lost interest when life started to become difficult? Why did they lose interest?

4. What does the Swamp of Despair represent? How can despair be dangerous in the life of a believer?

5. Because of his burden, Christian becomes more entrenched in the mud and is unable to pull himself out. In Psalm 40:12, David describes a place to be avoided because, once in it, it tends to become impossible to get out of without help. How do we get ourselves into these "muddy pit" situations that cling to us and prevent us from climbing out?

6. Who finally pulls Christian out of the swamp, and who does this man represent? God's desire is not for you to be stuck in the Swamp of Despair. Describe a time when God appointed someone to help you as you were struggling and felt there was no hope.

7. Before pulling Christian out of the swamp, Help asks him why he didn't just take the steps that had been placed in the middle of the swamp. These reliable steps represent the promises of God. Reflect on Psalm 37:23–24. What is God's promise to you in these verses?

The Advice of Worldly Wiseman

1. As Christian gets back on the right path, he's soon approached by Mr. Worldly Wiseman. Who does Wiseman represent in this story?

2. What strategies does Worldly Wiseman use to convince Christian to take a different path? Read Colossians 2:8. The Greek word for captive implies being kidnapped or taken hostage. Provide some examples by which we can be taken captive by human philosophies or the wisdom of the day.

3. Whom do Legality and Civility represent?

4. Worldly Wiseman provides Christian with an alternative way to remove his burden that's based on what man can do as opposed to what God can do. Read Galatians 3:1–5. Paul calls the Galatians foolish and reminds them that although they have received the Spirit, they are still trying to please God by observing the law. What are some ways in which we might try to please God by doing something other than doing so out of our love for Him?

In Search of Morality

1. What happens to Christian when he follows the advice of Worldly Wiseman?

2. In Christianity, legalism is when we place something that we do (an action or effort) above what Jesus did for us on the cross. This is essentially what Worldly Wiseman convinces Christian to do. He presents Christian with an option to relieve his sin (going to Mr. Legality) based on following a set of moral codes (living in the Village of Morality). What actions or efforts do we use to measure our spirituality? What are the consequences of legalism, and why is it such a serious issue?

3. Read Ephesians 2:8–10. What are the means by which we have been saved, and why is it important to embrace this if we are to truly live free?

4. What does Paul say the purpose of the law is in Galatians 3:10–12 and 3:19–22?

5. During his frustration and fear, Christian again encounters Evangelist. Why do you think Evangelist begins asking Christian a series of questions instead of just telling him where he went wrong? How might your discussions with friends and family who have "gotten off the right path" be different if you followed the same model?

6. After a series of probing questions, Evangelist then turns to Scripture to guide Christian to the truth. When God places us in a position to guide others, why is it so important to use God's Word as our compass?

7. What three things did Evangelist say Christian must hate about Worldly Wiseman? How did Christian react to Evangelist's counsel?

8. Both Evangelist and Christian regard sin as very serious. What is Jesus' solution for how to deal with the seriousness of sin in Matthew 18:7–9? How do you think this compares with how people regard sin today, even within the church?

Session 2: Chapter 2

Arrival at the Wicket Gate

1. After being rebuked by Evangelist for turning away from the right path, Christian is determined to get to the Wicket Gate safely without distraction from anything or anybody. What are some distractions, whether good or bad, that keep you from pursuing God at all costs?

2. Christian perseveres and arrives at the Wicket Gate, where he eagerly knocks several times to be let in. Read Matthew 7:7–8. What does the knocking teach us about man's responsibility in salvation?

3. Read John 10:9. Who does Goodwill represent?

4. Describe the basics of Christian's confession, despite his limited spiritual understanding, prior to entering the gate.

5. As Christian moves to enter the gate, Goodwill quickly yanks him through. He describes the enemy as being close by and well-fortified with an artillery of flaming arrows designed to kill those trying to enter the Wicket Gate. Read Ephesians 6:16. What is this scene dramatically illustrating with someone on the threshold of salvation?

6. Read Revelation 3:8. The church of Philadelphia was weak in some respects, yet they had remained faithful in the face of trials. Because of this, the Lord promises them an "open door" of blessing. What is the significance of Goodwill telling Christian that the open door cannot be shut?

7. The path Goodwill directs Christian to is straight and narrow. Read Matthew 7:13–14. Regarding our spiritual life, what is the difference between the path being straight and narrow or it being wide?

8. Most consider the decision of Christian to enter the Wicket Gate as the moment of his salvation. If this is so, why is his burden not immediately removed?

1. Goodwill directs Christian to the house of the Interpreter. Read John 14:26 and 15:26. What does the Interpreter represent? Read Ephesians 5:8–10. What is the significance of the Interpreter lighting the candle?

1st Room – The Portrait of the Preacher

1. The Interpreter leads Christian through the house and shows him spiritual realities illustrated in each room. The first room contained a portrait of the preacher, who is the only one authorized to be Christian's guide on his journey. Read 2 Peter 2:1–2. Why is it important that a new believer be taught to recognize a true minister of the gospel before anything else?

2. Match the following verses with the attributes of the preacher.

___ His eyes are looking heavenward.   a. 2 Timothy 4:7–8

___ He speaks the law of truth.   b. Titus 1:9

___ The world is behind his back.   c. 1 Corinthians 4:15

___ Pleads for reconciliation with God.   d. Ephesians 4:11–13

___ He has a gold crown over his head.   e. Colossians 3:2

___ He can produce children.   f. Romans 12:2

___ He nourishes those children.   g. 2 Corinthians 5:20

___ He preaches the truth.   h. Ephesians 4:25

2nd Room – The Dusty Room

1. In the second room, Christian watches as the doctrine of law and grace unfolds before him. Identify what each phrase represents below and the biblical truth it conveys.

a. The parlor (Jeremiah 17:9)

b. The dust (Romans 5:12)

c. The first sweeper (Romans 5:20)

d. The young lady (Titus 3:5)

2. Christian had already been exposed to legalistic assault when he ventured off the path to the mountain. Now, as a new believer, why do you think it's important that he's reminded yet again how the law and grace work together in a believer's life?

3rd Room – Passion and Patience

1. In the third room, Christian observes two children, Passion and Patience, and their reactions to the wishes of their governor. Describe the mannerisms of both children and whom they represent.

Passion –

Patience –

2. Why does Passion laugh and mock Patience? In Luke 16:25, how did the rich man's disregard for the pauper Lazarus play out in eternity?

3. Patience sat in the chair, holding back and watching Passion indulge in the immediate pleasure and satisfaction of his treasure. When do you find it most difficult to be patient and deny your passion while at the same time watching others find immediate pleasure in worldly desires?

4. What eventually happens to Passion, and what can we learn from his mistake? What does Jesus teach us in Matthew 6:19–20 about placing our hope and security in our possessions?

5. Our culture has lost touch with patience. We want everything now and with the least possible effort. Yet developing patience is essential as we grow to become more like Christ. Read Philippians 2:12–13. What does Paul mean by "work out your own salvation?"

6. What do you think the Interpreter means by expressing the difficulty of our present situation when he states that our "natural desires" and "spiritual desires" are close neighbors?

4th Room – The Roaring Fire

1. In the fourth room, Christian is shown a fire roaring in a fireplace and a man trying to extinguish the fire while another is fueling it. What do the fireplace and the fire represent?

2. The devil and his evil forces represent the man attempting to extinguish the fire. How does the enemy seek to douse your godly enthusiasm?

3. Even though the fire is drenched with water, Christian is amazed to see it burning higher and hotter. Who is the man sustaining the fire on the other side of the wall? Read 2 Corinthians 4:6–7. Throughout this passage, Paul is conveying the message of weakness and power. Containers are weak, but God is strong. How does God use your weaknesses to show His power?

4. Read 2 Corinthians 12:9 and Philippians 2:12–13. Amid difficult times, what principle of grace is revealed here?

5th Room – The Palace

1. In the fifth room, the Interpreter takes Christian to see a beautiful palace representing the glory of heaven that had many people clothed in gold walking on top of it. Who might these people represent in 2 Timothy 4:7?

2. Who does the large group of men who desire to enter the palace but are afraid represent? Who does the company of men in armor guarding the palace entrance represent?

3. What are some modern-day reasons why many people consider the call of following God and the truth of Scripture but never actually follow through?

4. In James 4:4, James uses strong language, saying, "Friendship with the world is hatred towards God." What kind of friendship is James talking about? How does this compare with Jesus' statement in Matthew 6:24?

5. Read Acts 14:22 and Philippians 1:29. What do we learn from the valiant man who fights his way into the palace? What does Jesus mean about the Kingdom of God in Matthew 11:12 when He says that the violent take it by force?

6. The valiant man publicly professes that he is a true believer by taking the sword (the Word of God) and his helmet (salvation) and rushing toward the palace entrance with determination and perseverance. What valuable truths are found in this lesson that Christian will need to remember if he is to have a successful journey to the Celestial City?

7. Christian confidently smiles because he understands the meaning of this lesson and is ready to be on his way. Why do you think the Interpreter makes him wait a little longer? In what ways do we try to attack the world unprepared?

6th Room – The Caged Man

1. In the sixth room, Christian is disturbed by the sight of a caged man living in despair. What does an iron cage in a dark room represent in the life of a believer?

2. The dictionary defines despair as the complete loss or absence of hope, disheartenment, discouragement, desperation, distress, anguish, depression, misery, defeatism, pessimism, and even suicidal feelings. The cage the man is locked inside is made of iron to show how strong the bonds of despair can be upon the soul. Have you ever felt despair like this, and if so, how did you get through it?

3. We can speculate as to whether this person was a true believer trapped in despair or one who just claimed to be a believer but never truly made Christ the Lord of his life. Regardless, the man said that he got himself into such a horrible condition because he had neglected to watch and be on guard. What were some of the sins this man fell into? Read 1 Peter 5:8. What does it mean to be sober-minded and watchful? When is a Christian most vulnerable to the danger that the devil poses?

4. The man believed that the promises of God were no longer his to claim, and he convinced himself that God was denying him repentance; therefore he had no hope. Read Joel 2:12–13 and Psalm 51:17. What does true repentance look like, and what is God's response to it? In your experience, does your repentance look like a heart that has been torn like a garment, broken and contrite, or do you just go through the motions?

5. Before seeing the man in the cage, Christian was eager to go to battle against the enemy. What might this lesson have taught him?

7th Room – The Unprepared Dreamer

1. In the final room, Christian observes a man rising out of bed shaking and trembling because of a frightening dream. What about the dream frightened him? What about Christian's past might have allowed him to empathize with this man's agony?

2. Match the following verses with the teachings of the coming of Christ:

____ Trumpets & One coming in the clouds   a. John 5:28–29

____ The heavens ablaze   b. Rev. 20:11–15

____ A voice calling the dead forth   c. 2 Thess. 1:7–10

____ The books opening in judgment   d. 1 Thess. 4:16–17

3. As the stones began to shatter, the graves opened, and the dead came to life, the Man on the cloud ordered His angels to go among the resurrected to gather the chaff and the wheat. Read Matthew 3:11–12 and Matthew 13:30. Who do these two groups represent, and what is the fate of each?

Chaff –

Wheat –

4. The man awakes and is terrified of the greater realization that he is not prepared for God's judgment. The warning in his dream was an act of divine grace allowing him a second chance. Describe the various earthly reminders God might allow in our lives to get our attention. Have you ever had a similar experience? If so, explain.

5. Everything the Interpreter shows Christian is designed to teach him different aspects of the spiritual life and to make sure he stays on the right path while avoiding deceptive spirits along the way. Which room of the Interpreter's house do you find the most encouraging? Which room do you find the most disturbing?

Session 3: Chapter 3

Arrival at the Cross

1. As Christian begins his journey, the burden on his back is still weighing him down until he arrives at the cross. Many have speculated that Christian was saved when he entered earlier at the Wicket Gate, while others suggest he was saved when the burden rolled off his back at the cross. What do you think, and why? Why might a believer continue to carry his burdens after being saved?

2. Read Philippians 2:12–13. What does it mean to be saved if we still need to be working out our salvation? Does this mean you can lose your salvation?

3. Christian must travel up a small hill to the cross and then later up the Hill of Difficulty. What consistent struggles do you face that threaten to deter you from working out your salvation?

4. Describe Christian's experience when he lost his burden. In John 15:10–11 and Philippians 3:1, we are told to keep God's commands and then rejoice and remain in the Lord for our own safety. Why is continuing to carry our own burdens so dangerous to our spiritual health?

5. Describe the role of each of the three shining angels that appeared to Christian as he was relieved of his burden.

The First Angel (Romans 5:1)

The Second Angel (Zech. 3:3–5)

The Third Angel (Rev. 22:4) –

6. The sealed certificate for his journey is a symbol of Christian's assurance of salvation. In this certificate, God confirms that Christian's identity is now found in Him. Read Ephesians 1:13. What does it mean that believers have been sealed by the Holy Spirit? What does it mean to have assurance of salvation, and how can trusting in that change a person's life?

Simple, Lazy, and Arrogance

1. Christian is enthusiastic when he leaves the cross, having just experienced great blessing, deliverance, and a renewed sense of joyous assurance. Then he encounters three men, Simple, Lazy, and Arrogance, who have a very naïve attitude toward the world. Describe each of these men and what they represent.

Simple (Proverbs 1:32–33)

Lazy (Proverbs 6:1–11) –

Arrogance (Philippians 2:3)

2. Christian meets Simple, Lazy, and Arrogance early on in his spiritual life. They are asleep (spiritually ignorant), in chains (in bondage to sin), and lying down (not watchful or alert). What dangers threaten to undermine the walk of new believers as they begin their spiritual journey?

An Encounter with Formalism and Hypocrisy

1. Leaving Simple, Lazy, and Arrogance behind, Christian then meets two other travelers named Formalism and Hypocrisy on the Way. How do these two men get on the road? What is their defense for not entering at the Wicket Gate?

2. Formalism and Hypocrisy were convinced that their way was an acceptable shortcut, arguing, "What difference does it make how we get on the Way as long as we get on it?" How might someone make this same argument today?

3. Regarding religion, the word "formalism" means a strong attachment to external forms of worship and observances. The word "hypocrisy" is the practice of claiming to have moral standards or beliefs to which one's own behavior does not conform. How does 2 Timothy 3:5 describe someone who is a formalist? According to Matthew 6:2–5, whom does Hypocrisy represent in the church today?

4. Formalism and Hypocrisy claim that there's little difference between themselves and Christian. But after carefully probing and investigating their beliefs further, what conclusion does Christian come to?

5. Read John 10:1, 7–10. What scriptural basis does Christian use to inform the two men that they enter the Way illegally? What did he say would happen to them when they arrived at the Celestial City?

Climbing the Hill of Difficulty

1. What does the Hill of Difficulty represent in the life of the believer? According to James 1:2–5, 1 Peter 4:12–13, and 2 Corinthians 1:3–5 why might God allow difficulties in your life? What was the most difficult experience you encountered early on in your Christian life?

2. Unlike Formalism and Hypocrisy, Christian is determined not to let temporary difficulties sway him from choosing the right path. Read Matthew 7:14. What is the benefit of the narrow Way over all other paths? How do you make sure that you are on the right path?

3. Once you are on the right path, how do you stay on it and not become distracted by the noise in the world today? What distracts you from staying on the right path?

4. Christian goes from running to walking and then finally crawling up the Hill of Difficulty, emphasizing the stress that trials can have on the spirit. Read Psalm 23:1–3 and Matthew 11:28. What does the shady arbor represent in the life of a Christian? What did Christian do at the shady arbor that gave him encouragement?

5. Eventually, Christian becomes drowsy and slips into the very condition he had earlier found to be so deplorable in Simple, Lazy, and Arrogance. Read 1 Thessalonians 5:6–8. What sort of dangers might we encounter when we allow ourselves to fall into a "spiritual sleep"?

6. When Christian leaves the shady arbor, what does he leave behind? What does this represent in the Christian life?

The Fear of Nervousness and Mistrust

1. Describe Nervousness and Mistrust and their report to Christian.

2. Read Numbers 13:25–33. Moses sends twelve spies out on a mission, and after forty days, they return to report on what they saw in this exotic new land. All twelve observe and experience the same things, and yet two of them return with an account that is entirely different from that of the other ten. What is it that enables Joshua and Caleb to see the Promised Land through different eyes?

3. Share a time when fear caused you to miss out on a great opportunity. Read 2 Timothy 1:7 and Romans 8:31. What do these passages teach us about fear and faith?

4. How did Christian first respond to Nervousness and Mistrust's news of the lions, and how did he keep himself from panicking?

5. Read 2 Corinthians 10:5. How can we control the thousands of thoughts that enter our minds each day, and how can we take every thought captive?

6. How does Christian respond to the discovery that he has lost his certificate?

7. Christian was overcome with joy to find his certificate and was spiritually revived, reassured, and thankful but soon realized the price that was to be paid for his laziness. What does this event teach us about how our past sins and failures can have present consequences for our lives?

Session 4: Chapter 4

Arrival at the Palace Beautiful

1. As night approaches, Christian becomes afraid, but then, by the grace of God, he sees a place to rest. Read Matthew 16:18. What does the Palace Beautiful represent in the life of a Christian?

2. When Christian sees the palace, he hurries to get in but notices that the Way has narrowed and is guarded by the lions that had frightened away Nervousness and Mistrust. Read 1 Peter 5:8. What do the lions represent in this passage?

3. Though the lions may roar and appear menacing, the porter tells Christian not to fear them because they're chained. What encouragement does this give you to know that despite the opposition you face, God is still sovereign and in control?

4. Match the strategy that Satan uses against us with the appropriate verse below:

_____ He lies.   a. 2 Cor. 4:4

_____ He blinds our minds.   b. 1 Thess. 2:18

_____ He disguises himself.   c. 2 Cor. 11:3

_____ He tempts us to sin.   d. John 8:44

_____ He fights against us.   e. 2 Cor. 11:13–15

5. When Christian arrives unharmed at the gate, he's greeted by the porter, named Watchman. Read Isaiah 62:6. Who does Watchman represent in ancient Israel, and what is his role in this story? What would be the role of a watchman in the church today?

6. Before Christian is allowed to stay at the Palace, Watchman interviews him and then seeks the counsel of Discretion. Read Proverbs 2:11. Who does Discretion represent?

7. We should make every effort to proclaim the gospel to all that attend church. However, why might it be important to use discretion with those that are not yet members of the family or body of Christ?

8. Once Discretion concludes that Christian's profession of faith is real, she introduces him to other family members, who welcome him warmly into the house. Although there is no scriptural mandate for official church membership, why might it be important to identify ourselves with a local body of believers? Read Philippians 2:2.

Answer Guide and Scripture References Available at **www.BrownChairBooks.com**

An Interview with Piety, Prudence, and Charity

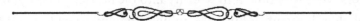

1. After interviewing Christian and being convinced that his testimony is sincere, Watchman and Discretion invite him into the house, where he shares his pilgrimage story in more detail. Why is sharing our story with other believers so important? Whose story have you found particularly encouraging, and why?

2. Piety is defined as devotion to God shown by your worship and behavior. Who does Piety represent in this story? What type of questions does Piety ask to assess the depth of Christian's spiritual understanding and maturity?

3. Read 2 Peter 1:5–7. What did Peter urge his readers to add to their faith? Which of these character qualities do you find most difficult to practice? Which ones do you consider the most important to add to your faith? Why?

4. To be prudent is to live and act with discretion and to exercise good judgment. Who does Prudence represent in the story? What type of questions does Prudence ask, and why does she continue to probe?

5. Read Proverbs 10:19, 12:16, 13:16, 14:15, and 22:3. What benefit do these verses offer the believer that practices prudence?

6. Prudence asks Christian if he's still drawn to his former way of life. Christian admits that he struggles and feels shame and disgust about certain things, but he truly desires now to do what is right. Read Romans 7:16–19. Is Paul giving believers an excuse to sin and removing any hope of walking in godliness?

7. What is Christian's strategy to guard against carnal thoughts? How do you guard against your carnal thoughts?

.

8. The word charity in the Bible nearly always means unconditional love. Who does Charity represent in this story? What does her line of questioning lead Christian to discover?

9. What does Paul say that our motivation for love (charity) must be in 1 Corinthians 13:1? What becomes of our motivations if they are exercised without love? How can we tell whether one's motivation is really love?

10. Charity voices her concern about Christian arriving at the house alone. He is brokenhearted because he had warned his family repeatedly of the danger of staying behind and begged them to come, but they would not listen. What encouragement does Charity offer him? Do you feel as though you have done all you can to lead your loved ones to Christ?

Suiting Up for Battle

1. After Prudence, Piety, and Charity question Christian and examine his life and testimony, they invite him to join the family for a meal. What do you think Bunyan intended for this supper to represent? What is the main topic of conversation around the table?

2. The fellowship of believers, the breaking of bread, and prayer have been steadfast practices since the earliest days of the church (Acts 2:42). Read 1 Corinthians 11:23–29. Who celebrates the Lord's Supper, when do they celebrate it, and for what purpose?

3. Following supper, they continue the conversation until late in the evening, at which time they pray and Christian retires to a spacious bedroom named Peace. Read Psalm 4:8 and John 14:27. What is the significance of going to sleep in a room named Peace? Do you go to sleep at night feeling at peace? What causes you to lose your peace?

4. After a restful night in the chamber of Peace, Christian is asked to stay and see the rarities of the house. What room is he taken to first, and what does it represent in the life of a Christian? What significance might there be to him going to the study in the morning? (Read Psalm 5:3, Psalm 88:13, and Psalm 119:147)

5. The study of Scripture is vital to the formation of a healthy spiritual life. What did you depend on for guidance in life prior to becoming a Christian? How did that work for you? How does Paul describe the benefits of being guided by Scripture in 2 Timothy 3:16?

6. An armory is a storage place for weapons and war equipment and is where military personnel are trained. What is the purpose of the armory in the house, and what sort of provisions are found there?

7. Read 2 Corinthians 10:3–4 and Ephesians 6:10–18. What is the real war taking place in the world? Who is it between? What is the purpose of the armor? What does it mean to stand firm, and what are we standing firm against?

8. Christian is asked to stay one more day so that he might go to the palace roof and get a glimpse of the Delectable Mountains. Whereas the Palace Beautiful represents the church from the vantage point of a new believer still learning and growing in knowledge and faith, the Delectable Mountains (where Christian will eventually be) represents the church from the vantage point of a more mature believer. What truth about the Christian life is illustrated by this event?

9. Christian is accompanied down the hill by Discretion, Piety, Charity, and Prudence as they rehearse and remind Christian of the truth and promises of God's Word. What point is being made here about the significance of the support of fellow believers when we enter times of difficulty and distress?

10. Christian seems to be more equipped than at any other time in his journey, so why do you think descending the mountain can be more dangerous than going up? What sort of "stumbles" are we susceptible to? According to Psalm 94:17–18, what should be our first response when we begin to stumble?

Session 5: Chapter 5
The Battle with Apollyon

1. Why do you think Bunyan had Christian enter the Valley of Humiliation following his experience at the Palace Beautiful? What does the Valley of Humiliation represent in the life of a believer?

2. How did God help Paul maintain an appropriate level of humility in 2 Corinthians 12:7–10? How has God helped you to maintain an appropriate level of humility?

3. In the valley, Christian quickly encounters the beast Apollyon. According to the text and Revelation 9:1–11, describe Apollyon. Who does he represent and what are his intentions with Christian?

4. When Christian first sees Apollyon, he considers retreating. However, he resolves to move forward because he realizes that he has no armor for his back, which would make him even more vulnerable to attack. Why in the list of spiritual armor is there no back plate? According to Ephesians 6:14–15 and James 4:7, what might God want us to do instead?

5. What spiritual battles do you fight in your day-to-day life? How does the enemy most often attack you?

6. What methods and arguments does Apollyon use in his attempt to discourage Christian and convince him to turn back to him?

7. When Apollyon tries to shame Christian by accusing him of sin and unfaithfulness, how does Christian respond? How might Christian have responded to the accusations if he did not have a firm grasp on his forgiveness in Christ?

8. Christian's answers to Apollyon's accusations send the beast into a fierce rage, and the confrontation escalates into full-grown spiritual warfare. Read Proverbs 4:23 and Ephesians 6:16. Why did Apollyon aim his first arrow at Christian's chest, and how did Christian respond?

9. What can we learn about spiritual warfare from the fact that Christian battled Apollyon for more than half a day, and why is it important not to give up?

10. As the battle continues, Apollyon is successful in wounding Christian. Why might these three areas, the head (Romans 12:2), the hand (1 Corinthians 15:2), and the foot (Romans 10:15), have been strategic points of injury for Apollyon?

11. As Apollyon sees Christian growing weaker, he comes at him with full force and fury. During the battle, Christian's sword flies out of his hand. What impression does this give you about the importance of God's Word in spiritual warfare?

12. It is only when Christian takes up the double-edged sword again that the tide of the battle turns. A double-edged sword has both edges sharpened. It is a very lethal weapon since it can be used with thrusts and swipes in any direction with equal effectiveness. With this understanding, what does Paul mean when he says the Word of God is sharper than any double-edged sword in Hebrews 4:12? How does Christian finally defeat Apollyon?

13. When the battle is over and Apollyon has fled, Christian expresses his thanksgiving with a song of praise, receives leaves from the Tree of Life to heal his wounds, and is refreshed by the bread and wine. What is Bunyan attempting to illustrate with this imagery?

Entering the Valley of the Shadow of Death

1. After Christian leaves the Valley of Humiliation, he enters an even darker and more fearful place called the Valley of the Shadow of Death. Modern translations more accurately translate this valley found in Psalm 23:4 as the "dark valley." What does this dark valley represent in the life of a Christian?

2. Christian enters this dark valley having just battled Apollyon. Describe a time in your life when one trial led to an even worse one, leaving you feeling confused, alone, or abandoned. In what ways do we become vulnerable during dark times? Regardless of circumstances, what simple truth about the Valley of the Shadow of Death should we remember in Psalm 23:4, and how does Paul rephrase it in 2 Corinthians 4:8–9?

3. As Christian crosses the boundary between the valleys, he meets two men who have turned back in fear and are encouraging Christian to do the same. These men represent the descendants of the ten spies in Numbers 13:25–32 and 14:1–4 who lacked faith and gave a bad report to Moses. How did the Israelites respond to this report? How does Christian respond to the report given him? Why do you think Bunyan made the road to the Celestial City pass through this valley?

4. In the valley ahead, Christian sees a narrow and safe path surrounded by dangerous conditions on both sides. What does the ditch and quagmire represent in the life of a Christian?

Ditch – Matthew 15:12–14

Quagmire – Psalm 69:14–15

5. When Christian tries too hard to avoid one of these hazards, he is in danger of falling into the other. In other words, when he exposes his sin with truth (the ditch), he is in danger of being overwhelmed with guilt (the quagmire). How do we find balance and stay safely on the path?

6. When Christian reaches the middle of the valley and comes near the mouth of Hell, he is tormented with voices of terror and temptation. What sort of vivid pictures of Hell does Bunyan portray? How does Jesus describe Hell in Matthew 13:41–42 and 25:30 as well as in Luke 16:22–24?

7. Why did Christian change his mode of defense from his sword to all-prayer? Paul instructs us to constantly be praying in the Spirit on *all* occasions with *all* kinds of prayers and requests in Ephesians 6:18 and 1 Thessalonians 5:17. Do you struggle to pray without ceasing on all occasions with all kinds of prayers and requests?

8. What sort of attack did the devil launch upon Christian's mind? In dark times, we can often experience unwanted thoughts and temptations that seem to come from nowhere. Satan is playing a vicious, intense, and unfair battle for our minds. Read 2 Corinthians 10:3–5 and Romans 12:2 and reflect on how a believer can guard against these attacks and trials of the mind.

9. What gave Christian encouragement while he plodded on through the darkness? Describe a time when the encouragement of another gave you hope as you walked through a difficult time.

10. As the sun begins to rise, Christian gains a better perspective on the dangers from which God has protected him as well as being able to better discern and anticipate what might lie ahead. How does the light of God's Word (Psalm 119:105) and a new day help us make better sense of long, difficult, and dark trials?

11. When Christian reached the end of the valley, he passed by a cave where two giants, Pope and Pagan, lived. Pagan represents the worship of many gods and had been dead for many years. Pope represents the Roman Catholic Church and was once powerful and formidable but was now weak and feeble. Both giants, in their day, had been responsible for persecuting pilgrims and sending many to their death. Read Hebrews 11:32–12:1. List some of the things that people of faith have endured. What did these "heroes of the faith" gain?

Session 6: Chapter 6

Temptation, Discontentment, and Shame

1. As Christian emerges from the Valley of the Shadow of Death, he spots his good friend Faithful. What progression in the Christian walk is Bunyan illustrating by the fact that Faithful was ahead of Christian on the path? Why would Faithful not wait for Christian to catch up?

2. Christian knows that he must pick up the pace if he is to catch up to Faithful. What does our "picking up the pace" in regard to spiritual growth involve? Christian catches up to Faithful and then becomes proud when he passes him on the path. What warning do 1 Corinthians 10:12 and Proverbs 16:18 offer against spiritual pride?

3. Christian learns from Faithful that his testimony and warnings did have an impact on the City of Destruction. What else did he learn regarding his old friend Pliable, who had abandoned him in the Swamp of Despair? How did the townspeople respond to Pliable returning home? Why was Pliable worse off than he was before?

4. Faithful went on to describe a series of temptations that he experienced after escaping the City of Destruction. Define the word "wanton." What temptation does Wanton represent? How does Wanton lure Faithful into her snare?

5. Using Job 31:1, Psalm 119:11, and Matthew 5:28–30, describe how Faithful keeps himself from succumbing to Wanton's temptation. How does Wanton tempt believers today, and what promises does she make?

6. When Faithful arrives at the foot of the Hill of Difficulty, he meets a very old man named Adam the First. According to Romans 6:6, who does this old man represent? How does he go about tempting Faithful to leave the path and come with him?

7. Using 1 John 2:15–16 as a metaphor for Adam's offer of the marriage of his daughters to Faithful, what three basic ways are we tempted by the world to choose our will over God's will? Elaborate on each of these and what that temptation might look like in your life. According to John, what does having a "love for the world" indicate about our relationship with God?

8. What was the warning that was written on Adam's forehead, found in Ephesians 4:22, that keeps Faithful from succumbing to temptation? Faithful learns that resisting the old man is hard. In Romans 7:22–24, Paul describes his own struggle with remaining in sin. How can fighting the sin inside us feel like we are being torn apart?

9. As Faithful nears the shady arbor while climbing the Hill of Difficulty, he encounters yet more opposition, from Moses. What does Moses represent, and what temptation does Faithful encounter? Why is Moses portrayed as beating Faithful severely, and why can't he stop? Read Romans 6:23 and James 2:10 for reference.

10. When Faithful was left for dead at the feet of Moses, he had no hope in his own ability to defeat Moses. How does he eventually escape from this temptation and death? Read Hebrews 3:3, 1 John 1:7, and Romans 8:1.

11. Next, Faithful meets Discontent in the Valley of Humiliation. What argument (or temptation) does Discontent use to try to persuade Faithful not to enter the valley? How does Faithful overcome the temptation?

12. When are you most at risk of becoming discontent? How does Paul instruct us to handle contentment in 1 Timothy 6:6–10, Hebrews 13:5, and Philippians 4:11–12?

13. After leaving Discontent, Faithful encounters Shame in the Valley of Humiliation. Define the word "shame." Based on the definition, why does Faithful believe Shame has the wrong name?

14. What arguments does Shame use against Faithful to make him feel ashamed of the gospel? What do the following passages say about our being ashamed of the gospel: Mark 8:38, Romans 1:16, Philippians 1:20, and 2 Timothy 1:12?

15. Using 1 Corinthians 1:26–29 and Luke 16:15, how does Faithful respond to Shame's arguments? Shame does not give up and continues to berate Faithful. Why is shame a foe that we must be on guard against?

The Hypocrisy of Talkative

1. As the men continue their journey, Faithful encounters a man named Talkative and strikes up a conversation with him. Why is Faithful so drawn to Talkative? What type of person are you most drawn to, and why?

2. At first, Talkative appears to have a lot of commendable qualities, and Faithful quickly becomes impressed with his fluent words and contagious enthusiasm. According to Ecclesiastes 5:3 and 10:14, what indicators does the Bible provide for recognizing a fool? Not everyone that talks a lot is in error. Where is the line between being overly suspicious and judgmental of a talkative person while not being gullible, naïve, and even deceived?

3. Faithful steps aside to speak privately with Christian about his new friend but finds that Christian is not impressed with Talkative because he knows the truth about him. What are some of the concerns Christian has about Talkative?

4. Even though Christian's assessment of Talkative may seem quite severe, his judgments and warnings are warranted. Read Matthew 12:34 and Matthew 18:6–7. How did Jesus respond to those in His day that lived in hypocrisy and led others astray? Do you think there are people in the church today that fit the description of Talkative? If so, in what way?

5. Christian is concerned that Talkative does not grasp the vital relationship between faith and works. Read Galatians 2:16, Ephesians 2:8–9, and James 2:14–26. Describe the relationship between faith and works. How does real faith affect a person's actions? How did James describe faith that has no accompanying works?

6. Now that his eyes are opened, Faithful is ready to be rid of Talkative. However, Christian counsels him to first do the responsible thing and speak with Talkative about the power of the gospel to change hearts and lives. What might Paul have been concerned about when he wrote Colossians 4:3–4 that would inhibit or hinder his clarity of speech or prevent him from proclaiming the gospel in the way he desired?

7. What was Talkative's first answer as to how a person can know whether they are truly saved, and how does Faithful respond? What three illustrations does Faithful use to explain the difference?

8. What was Talkative's second answer as to how a person can know whether they are truly saved, and how does Faithful respond? According to 1 Corinthians 13:1–2 and Psalm 119:34, what should knowledge that is accompanied with love compel us to do?

9. Faithful made the uncomfortable decision to confront Talkative about his ideas on faith, even though he suspected that Talkative might not listen or even refuse to answer. How willing are you to engage someone in a difficult conversation about faith when a more pleasant conversation would be much easier?

10. When Talkative resists Faithful's attempts to correct him, Faithful offers to provide an answer to the question of saving grace. Match Faithful's explanation of the nature of saving grace with the appropriate verse.

___ Conviction and repentance of sin   a. Matthew 5:6

___ A confession of faith in Christ   b. Romans 15:13

___ A hunger and thirst for righteousness   c. Philippians 1:27

___ A struggle between the old and new man   d. Acts 4:12

___ The peace of knowing Christ   e. Philippians 2:4

___ A life that displays transformation to others   f. Psalm 40:8

___ A concern for friends and family   g. Romans 7:24

___ A submission of the heart to God's Word   h. John 16:8 ESV

11. After Faithful presents the truth of salvation, what questions does he use to encourage Talkative to evaluate his own life? How does Talkative respond?

12. Do you think many in our day would agree with Talkative that Faithful was being too judgmental and unkind? If so, how? Many people read Matthew 7:1–5 and say that Jesus said not to judge. However, what might a closer examination reveal?

13. After Talkative departs, Christian also commends Faithful for doing the right thing by speaking plainly to Talkative and counsels Faithful to let him go. What does 1 Timothy 6:3–5 counsel us to do with those that claim Christ but cling to sin?

Evangelist Warns of the Coming Tribulation

1. As Christian and Faithful near the end of the wilderness, they see a friend coming and recognize him as Evangelist. On what other occasions did Evangelist appear to Christian?

2. Christian and Faithful are excited to see Evangelist since he was instrumental in sharing the gospel with both of them. As he returns to see how they are doing on their journey, he rejoices to hear that even though they've experienced some dark trials, they were victorious and persevered. Read 3 John 4 and John 4:36 and discuss a time when you have rejoiced over someone's testimony with whom you were instrumental in sharing the gospel.

3. Evangelist provided biblical counsel and encouragement for Christian and Faithful and told them to hold on and not give up on the Christian life. Read Galatians 6:9. When are we most in danger of becoming weary of doing good in the Christian life? According to Mark 14:38, why do we become weary? Discuss a time in your life when you became weary of trying to do good.

4. Using Paul's athletic illustration of a race in 1 Corinthians 9:24–27 and 2 Timothy 4:8, Evangelist instructs Christian and Faithful to keep focused on the crown and not get distracted. Evaluate where you are in the race. Are you jogging along, or are you running to win the crown that will last? What things might be coming between you and the crown, and what would it take for you to give those things up? What is your training plan to win the race?

5. Read Hebrews 12:4. What do you think Evangelist means when he tells Christian and Faithful that they are "not yet out of the gun-shot range of the devil and have not resisted sin to the point of shedding their own blood"?

6. Knowing that Evangelist is a prophet, Christian invites him to journey with them a while and prepare them for future events. What warnings does he give? What encouragements does he give? What encouragement do you get from reading James 1:12, Revelation 2:10, and John 16:33?

Session 7: Chapter 7

On Trial at Vanity Fair

1. In Ecclesiastes 1:2, Solomon relentlessly emphasizes that "all is vanity" that is "under the sun." In this context, the word "vanity" means "emptiness," "futility," "vapor," or "that which vanishes quickly and leaves nothing behind." As you look around at the world today, what appears to you to be vanity? How should this change your perspective on life?

2. What does the town of Vanity Fair represent? How is Vanity Fair like the state of the world today?

3. Bunyan describes the fair as being very old, suggesting its origins were at the Garden of Eden, where Adam and Eve were first tempted and enticed to disobey God. Why was it important for Bunyan to emphasize and establish that the origins of the fair date back to the beginning of creation? Why do you think the fair is also described as lasting all year long?

4. We learn that the fair is corrupt by the description of the goods sold, the profane occupations, and the complete lawlessness. It's important to understand that not everything included at the fair is bad (houses, land, trades, wives, husbands, children, silver, gold, pearls, and precious stones). According to 1 Corinthians 6:12 and James 4:3, how can something that's inherently good become something bad? What good thing has become a stumbling block in your life, and how do you guard your heart against it?

5. The fair is international, with avenues and streets all named after countries and kingdoms and filled with extravagant and desirable goods. How does God view all the nations and cultures of the world in Isaiah 40:17?

6. Vanity Fair is representative of the world in which we are born into. As such, the only way to get to the next world, the Celestial City, is for us to pass through this world. Read John 15:19 and 17:14–16. What do you think it means to be "in" this world but not "of" it?

7. How are Christian and Faithful different from the people of Vanity Fair? Have you ever appeared different than others because of your faith? Explain.

8. After being ridiculed for looking away from worthless things at the fair, Christian and Faithful told one merchant they would buy the truth. Read Proverbs 23:23. What do you think it means to buy the truth and not sell it? What can the truth cost you?

9. Once apprehended, Christian and Faithful remain calm and do not panic or counterattack their abusers. Instead, with wisdom and patience, they endure intense persecution and public humiliation. In Philippians 1:21–24, what comfort did Paul find in his suffering while imprisoned in a Roman jail?

10. Christian and Faithful's witness had a positive impact on some men at the fair who began to feel compassion for them and a desire for the truth. How did Paul's faithful witness in times of difficulty open the door to the gospel for others in Philippians 1:12–14? How do you find the strength to love someone who has hurt (or is hurting) you?

11. Christian and Faithful were brought before the judge, Lord Hate-good, to face charges of disturbing the peace and dividing the town by swaying some to accept their views. How does Faithful respond to this indictment?

12. Peter and John were arrested for preaching about Jesus and put in jail. The religious authorities were determined to stop them. How did they respond to their accusers in Acts 4:19–20 and 5:29? If governmental authorities, who could tax, imprison, or even have you executed, told you to stop telling people about Jesus, what would you do? When is it right to disobey society's rules?

13. As the trial in Vanity Fair unfolds, Bunyan suggests that persecution and oppression of the church arise in the form of Envy, Superstition, and Flattery. Envy represents the town leaders who are jealous of the growing influence that Christian and Faithful are having on the town. In much the same way, how did the Jews respond when they saw the whole city coming together to hear the Word of God in Acts 13:44–45?

14. Superstition symbolizes religious, progressive churchgoers that believe there's more than one way to heaven, that Jesus Christ was just a good man, and that there's no hell. Christian and Faithful exposed these false beliefs embraced by Superstition, who then felt threatened when he heard the clear message of the Gospel. In John 14:6, Jesus declares Himself the only way to heaven, the only true measure of righteousness, and the source of both physical and spiritual life. What is our responsibility to oppose the progressive and empty religious systems and cults of the world?

15. Flatterer represents those that bow to social pressure to gain acceptance to make his own position seem more favorable. In this case, he pours on the flattery in his testimony against Faithful to receive the acceptance of the town's noblemen and the judge. Read Psalm 5:9, Proverbs 29:5, and Romans 16:18. How can you spot flattery as opposed to a genuine compliment? How does flattery affect us when we listen to it? How does flattery show a lack of trust in God?

16. The judge calls on a corrupt jury to deliver a guilty verdict, which they quickly do. For such a progressive and tolerant society as Vanity, they quickly become intolerant of Christian and Faithful's beliefs. How would you define tolerance of the Christian faith in today's politically correct world?

17. In contrast to Faithful's cruel and tragic death, what glorious behind-the-scenes pictures does Bunyan paint for us taken from 1 Thessalonians 4:16–17 and 2 Kings 2:11?

18. Faithful is lovingly ushered to the very gates of the Celestial City, while Christian is spared and remains behind to eventually press on in his journey. Read Romans 8:28 and Philippians 1:21–23. Why did Faithful have to die but Christian escaped? How is Faithful the most blessed one in this situation?

Session 8: Chapter 8
The Deceitfulness of Riches

1. After escaping Vanity Fair, Christian is joined by Hopeful, who is persuaded to become a pilgrim after witnessing the persecution of Christian and Faithful. Read Acts 7:54–8:2. What sort of lasting impression do you think the stoning of Stephen had on Paul's (formally Saul) life and his ministry?

2. Hopeful symbolizes the importance of Christian fellowship and pressing forward with hope despite circumstances. What hope does Jeremiah 29:11 offer to those that are experiencing suffering?

3. Not long into their journey, Christian and Hopeful overtake another traveler, named Mr. By-Ends from Fair-Speech. The word "by-ends" can be defined as having selfish ambition or motives. How would you describe Mr. By-Ends? What type of person might By-Ends represent in the church today?

4. By-Ends is not ashamed of his religion or opposed to being identified with Christ. In fact, he describes his religion as one that is relaxed and flexible to avoid persecution and also refined and elegant so as to avoid personal hardship. In what ways might someone today pervert, exploit, or abuse religion as a means to an end?

5. Christian places conditions on By-Ends if he should choose to travel with them, but By-Ends becomes offended and decides to part ways. According to Matthew 16:24–26, what does Jesus say true discipleship involves? Why might some be offended (like the rich young ruler in Matthew 19) by this teaching of Jesus?

6. Not long after parting ways with Christian and Hopeful, By-Ends is joined by Mr. Hold-the-World, Mr. Money-Love, and Mr. Save-All. Who were these men, and what was their relation to By-Ends?

7. As their conversation unfolds, the four men begin to legitimize their claims as Christians by rationalizing their own sin. To make the point, By-Ends asks, "Is it right for a minister or businessman to use religion in the pursuit of personal gain?" What four reasons does Money-Love offer to validate a minister's desire to modify his religion in order to pursue the higher-paying position?

8. What four reasons does Money-Love offer to validate a businessman's motivation to modify his religion as a means to expand the opportunity in his market?

9. Why might some find Money-Love's reasoning appealing? Why does 1 John 2:15–17 not give us the option to be partially committed both to God and to the world? Does "not loving the world" mean that it's wrong for a Christian to want to succeed in business or a career? Why or why not?

10. Convinced of the soundness of Money-Love's reasoning and that no one could refute it, By-Ends and his friends devise a plan to confront Christian and Hopeful. Christian easily sees through the superficiality of their questioning and counters by first pointing to John 6:26–27. What does Jesus say the motivation was for the people following him? What should our attitude be toward spiritual rewards and material benefits?

11. As Christian continues, what four additional biblical stories does he provide for rejecting their views of religion? Read Genesis 34:20–24, Luke 20:46–47, Matthew 26:14–16, and Acts 8:19–22.

The Snare of the Silver Mine

1. After leaving By-Ends and his friends, Christian and Hopeful arrive at the plain of Ease. What does Ease represent in the Christian life? What lesson do we learn from the fact that the pilgrims did not enjoy the comforts of Ease for very long but passed through it rather quickly?

2. After crossing the plain, the two men came to a little hill called Lucre, where there was a silver mine. The term "lucre" is Latin for "gain" and is used throughout Scripture to refer to greed, as in 1 Timothy 3:3 (KJV), "not greedy of filthy lucre." What would the hill of Lucre represent in the Christian life? Bunyan describes the hill as little to emphasize our perception of our desire for money as harmless and relatively acceptable—at least compared to other, more egregious sins. According to Deuteronomy 8:10–14 what is the temptation or danger that we fall into when we focus on obtaining wealth and prosperity?

3. As Christian and Hopeful near the mine, they are beckoned by a notorious person named Demas to come to see its marvels. Read Philemon 1:23–24, Colossians 4:14, and 2 Timothy 4:10. What is Demas's story in Scripture, and what does Paul say happened to him later in his ministry? Who represents Demas in the church today?

4. Demas tries to get Christian and Hopeful to turn aside from the straight and narrow path and pursue riches. Do you think it is a sin to want a nicer house, furniture, car, clothes, etc.? Why or why not? How do we balance such desires considering 1 Timothy 6:9–10? Should Christians not pursue making a profit?

5. Hopeful is curious and wants to go examine the mine, but Christian is not persuaded and recognizes the danger. What has Christian heard about both the mine and Demas that keeps him firm and resolute to stay on the Way? Read 2 Kings 5:20 and Matthew 26:14–15. Who does Christian compare Demas to?

6. What happened to By-Ends and his friends as they came by? Read Matthew 6:19–21. What warning should be taken away from this account?

A Monumental Warning

1. Shortly after passing the silver mine, Christian and Hopeful come upon a strange monument revealed to be Lot's wife. Briefly summarize the story of Lot's wife as found in Genesis 19.

2. Hopeful feels foolish for wanting to go to the mine and realizes that he deserves the same punishment as Lot's wife, yet he was spared. Why do you think Hopeful's life was spared while Lot's wife perished? Read Matthew 6:21. How might the condition of their hearts have played into their punishment?

3. In Numbers 16, a Levite named Korah and his clan members perished because they challenged Moses' leadership by demanding the status of priesthood all while ignoring the detailed instructions that the Lord had spoken through Moses regarding the distinctions between the priests and Levites. In Numbers 26:9–10, it is said that Korah and his clan members' deaths served as a warning to others. God wants us to learn from our own mistakes as well as the mistakes of others. What mistakes have you witnessed that have served as a warning to you, and why? Do you think our culture takes the warnings of sin seriously? Why or why not?

4. The pillar stood within sight of the mine as a warning, yet By-Ends and his friends ignored it. Read 1 Corinthians 10:12. Why might we sometimes ignore or discount warning signs that have been placed along our path?

5. Why did Christian and Hopeful think it was important to remember Lot's wife? What is Jesus teaching us in Luke 17:23–33 when He tells us to remember Lot's wife?

6. Consider the illustration of pick-pocketers and purse stealers committing their crime in the presence of a judge. Read Romans 1:28–32. What happens to a man or society that has the knowledge of the judgment of sin from a good and righteous God but does not consider it worthwhile to obey Him? What does it mean that "God gave them over"?

Session 9: Chapter 9

Taking the Easy Path

1. Read Psalm 23:2–3 and Revelation 22:1–2. What does the River of God represent in the life of a believer? When have you experienced a time such as this?

2. Christian and Hopeful resume the journey but are saddened to discover that the river is no longer close by. Now the Way is rough, their feet are sore, and they are discouraged until they arrive at By-Path meadow. What do this meadow and the steps leading into it represent in the life of a believer? When we become discouraged in our walk with Christ, what makes leaving the Way seem so appealing?

3. Sometimes we are our own worst enemy. Christian and Hopeful gained confidence after escaping Vanity Fair, recognizing the folly of By-Ends, rebuking the temptation of Demas, and heeding the warning of Lot's wife. According to Proverbs 3:5–6, Proverbs 14:12, and Isaiah 55:8–9, what is the danger in becoming too confident in our own wisdom, past experiences, and abilities? Give some examples that illustrate how people often follow what seems right to them rather than following God's Word.

4. When Christian and Hopeful first entered By-Path meadow, they found it much easier and experienced some pleasure and relief. They even became more confident that they had made the right choice after receiving assurance from Vain-Confidence. What happens that makes them realize their error? Who does Vain-Confidence represent in our world today?

5. When Christian realizes his error and that he has placed Hopeful in danger by straying from the Way, he quickly repents. Most of the time when an apology is offered in any relationship, there is an expectation of receiving forgiveness. Hopeful willingly forgives Christian and tells him that this will be for their good. What occurs when an apology is given but forgiveness is not offered?

6. Christian demonstrates true repentance—a repentance born of godly grief. How does Paul describe such repentance in 2 Corinthians 7:10–11? What is the difference between worldly and godly sorrow? How do you know which one a person is expressing?

7. During Christian and Hopeful's dispute over leadership, they hear a voice encouraging their repentance and directing them to return to the Way. Read 2 Timothy 3:16–17. When we stray from God's clear path for our lives, what is essential to repentance and restoration to the right path?

Trapped in Doubting Castle

1. Why did Christian and Hopeful find it both difficult and exhausting trying to get back on the Way? In our own lives, why might returning to a godly lifestyle seem exhausting after being wayward for a time?

2. The pilgrims soon discover they are trespassing on the grounds of Doubting Castle and are captured by its owner, Giant Despair. After winning so many other battles against the likes of Apollyon and others, why do you think Christian is now powerless against the giant, not even able to draw his sword?

3. What does the dungeon of Doubting Castle and Giant Despair represent in the life of a Christian? How does David describe his feelings of guilt in Psalm 32:3–4?

4. Even after trying to do the right thing, Christian is riddled with guilt, overwhelmed with doubts, and bound by despair in the dungeon. He knows it was his error that endangered both him and Hopeful. List some examples of how our own bad decisions, even after repentance, can still have a negative impact the lives of others.

5. In Bunyan's day, the term diffidence meant timidity and lack of trust. Giant Despair and his wife, Diffidence, plan their attacks at night, when there is no light. In each circumstance, she sends Despair to beat and abuse Christian and Hopeful. How do distrust and despair work together to beat us down and overwhelm us with guilt and remorse? According to Proverbs 3:21–26, why should we never lose sight of the wisdom of God's truth?

6. After beating them, Giant Despair advises Christian and Hopeful to take their own lives. Christian is so discouraged that he sees only two options: live in bondage to the giant or commit suicide and die. What might Christian have been overlooking according to Romans 8:37, Matthew 19:26, and Jeremiah 32:17?

7. What arguments against committing suicide did Hopeful use in counseling Christian? Have you ever counseled someone that was contemplating suicide? Share your experience and what arguments you might have used to convince them otherwise.

8. Christian and Hopeful eagerly plead for their freedom only to be met with what seems to be the giant's final assault. Yet, in that very moment, their raging captor falls into a seizure when exposed to a sunny day. Read John 1:5. What point is Bunyan making about the giant not being able to tolerate light?

9. Despite Hopeful's reassurance, the darkness returns, and Christian once again feels the weight of depression while trapped in the misery of Doubting Castle with no end in sight. What does Hopeful say to encourage Christian this time? Read Psalm 77:11–12 and Hebrews 10:32. Why is the remembrance of former spiritual conquests essential to overcoming depression?

10. Christian and Hopeful suffered in the misery of Doubting Castle from Wednesday through Saturday until they redirected their energy and began to pray. In James 1:5–8, we are commanded to pray without doubting. What does it look like to pray with doubt? What or who are we doubting? Explain the description that James gives us of a doubtful asker.

11. At daybreak, following a night of prayer, Christian remembers that he possesses a key close to his heart, called Promise, that will open any lock in Doubting Castle. What does the key represent, and what happens to Christian's outlook when he realizes he possesses it? Why is it so important to store the Word of God in our hearts, and what does this involve?

12. What is Bunyan suggesting from the fact that there was more than one gate to open and one of them was very hard?

13. Once the pilgrims were safely back on the Way, what plans did they make? Do you view your own experiences, struggles, and failures as useful in warning others of danger?

14. Have you ever experienced a time of doubt and despair in your life? Did Christian and Hopeful's imprisonment by Giant Despair resonate with your own experience? If so, how? How did you escape?

Session 10: Chapter 10

The Shepherds in the Mountains

1. After Christian and Hopeful escape Doubting Castle, they continue their journey, ascending the Delectable Mountains. Bunyan's description of the Delectable Mountains most likely represents the church. When did Christian last see these mountains? How is Christian's perspective of the mountains different than before? How might your perspective of church change as you mature as a Christian?

2. According to Acts 20:28 and 1 Peter 5:2–3, who might the shepherds and the sheep represent?

3. Christian and Hopeful met four shepherds, named Knowledge, Experience, Watchful, and Sincere. Define these four qualities as they relate to the characteristics of a pastor and why each is important in ministry.

Knowledge (Romans 15:14, Titus 1:9–11) –

Experience (1 Timothy 3:6) –

Watchful (Acts 20:28) –

Sincerity (1 Corinthians 13:1) –

4. After inviting them to stay, the shepherds take Christian and Hopeful the next day to the top of a hill called Error. Describe this hill. Read 1 Timothy 1:18–20 and 2 Timothy 2:17–18. Who were Hymenaeus and Philetus, and what are they examples of today? If each one of these hills were to represent a sermon, what is the sermon (or warning) of this hill according to 2 Peter 2:1?

5. The shepherds then lead Christian and Hopeful to the top of a hill called Caution, and they are told to look back. Describe what they see here. Read Proverbs 21:16. What is the sermon or warning the pilgrims receive about wandering off the path? How do discouragement and despair keep us blinded to the truth?

6. From this experience, Christian and Hopeful are overwhelmed with sadness and tears. Have you ever been in a church service or reading God's Word and suddenly become overwhelmed with sadness or regret due to some past sin? According to Hebrews 4:12–13, why do you think that is, and what benefit, if any, do we receive from remembering past mistakes?

7. As the shepherds continue guiding the pilgrims, they show them a door in the hillside. What do Christian and Hopeful see as they look in, and what does this place represent according to Revelation 20:10–15? What is the sermon or warning to the pilgrims about professing faith in Christ?

8. The shepherds emphasize the seriousness of sin by providing biblical examples of those that appeared to be among the faithful but were later found to be hypocrites. Read Matthew 15:7–8. Are there areas in your life where Jesus might say that you are being a hypocrite? What do Christian and Hopeful rightly conclude it will take to finish the journey?

9. After the shepherds show Christian and Hopeful all three warnings, they take them to the top of a hill called Clear. What do they see here through the shepherds' perspective glass that gives them hope? The perspective glass represents God's Word providing a glimpse of the joy for those that persevere in their walk with Christ. Why do their hands shake as they look through the glass? Read 1 Corinthians 13:12. What are some things you "see in a mirror dimly" now that you someday hope to see more clearly?

An Encounter with Ignorance

1. As the two pilgrims descend from the mountains, they encounter a "very lively young man" from the country of Conceit (self-satisfaction) entering the Way by a crooked path. Compare and contrast how both Christian and Ignorance entered the Way, considering where they entered, their demeanor, etc.

2. Christian appears to be familiar with the country of Conceit and questions Ignorance as to how he expects to gain entrance to the Celestial City. What is Ignorance's response, and where does his confidence seem to be placed?

3. What is Jesus' response in Luke 18:18–22 as to whether a good life, good deeds, and keeping the law are enough for gaining entrance to heaven? Have you ever had an encounter with anyone like Ignorance? Describe that experience.

4. This is not the first time Christian encounters others trying to enter the Way by their own works instead of at the Wicket Gate (Christ). Using John 10:1, how does Christian attempt to counsel Ignorance?

5. Ignorance is offended by Christian's counsel and tells him the Wicket Gate is too far away and the crooked path is closer, pleasant, and convenient. How would you respond to someone that has shown interest in the teachings of Christ but claims the biblical way of salvation seems awfully involved and difficult?

6. Christian and Hopeful see no point in continuing the conversation with Ignorance and decide to leave in hopes that he will think it over and eventually be open to further discussion. Read Proverbs 26:12. How do you know when to pursue a conversation about the gospel or to be patient and wait for another opportunity?

7. Christian and Hopeful enter a "very dark lane" and see a man bound with seven strong cords. Read Proverbs 4:19. What does the dark lane represent? What happens to the light of God's Word when our minds continue to pursue sin? Who does Turn-away represent in the church?

8. Turn-away is at the end of his days and is being led back to the mountains to hell. Turning away from God, rejecting the gospel, and pursuing a lifestyle of sin and disobedience seldom happen all at once. Identify the more subtle ways that it can happen.

The Assault on Little Faith

1. The tragic account of Turn-away reminds Christian about another story of a pilgrim named Little Faith. What type of Christian does Little Faith represent? Several times in the book of Matthew (6:30, 8:25–26, and 14:31–32), Jesus refers to those that have little faith. What is the difference between having little faith and unbelief?

2. Little Faith unwisely lets his guard down and falls asleep in the dangerous intersection of Dead Man's Lane and Broadway. In what areas of your life are you prone to let your guard down and become lazy, leaving your heart vulnerable to the world?

3. Little Faith soon encounters Faint Heart, Mistrust, and Guilt. Their attack on Little Faith is an illustration of what happens when a believer becomes spiritually lazy and places themselves in compromising situations that lead to temptation and sin. To be faint-hearted is to lack courage. According to 2 Corinthians 4:16–18, how can a believer not lose heart when becoming overwhelmed by life's struggles? How does keeping an eternal perspective help?

4. For a believer, to mistrust is to worry and doubt God's faithfulness, mercy, love, grace, power, and ability, which can lead to anxiety. In the Sermon on the Mount, Jesus made it clear that anxiety stems from a lack of faith and from a wrong focus on the things of this world instead of on the kingdom of God (Matthew 6:25–34). In what areas of your life do you find yourself most likely to experience anxiety? What does Paul say the answer to anxiety is in Philippians 4:6–7?

5. For a believer, the weight of guilt can bring a sense of condemnation, thoughts that God is angry with us, or even a lack of a sense of forgiveness. These feelings take away our peace and contentment and replace them with fear and agitation. Read Psalm 103:8–12. How should we handle those occasions when guilty feelings arise over sins already confessed?

6. When the thieves stole Little Faith's money, they robbed him of his comfort and peace. He was consumed with grief over his loss and left with no hope or assurance of his future and with barely enough money for the rest of his journey. Using Romans 8:28, how would you go about mentoring a spiritually weak believer who's dealing with a tough life situation and is scared and anxious and perhaps has feelings of guilt with no hope for the future?

7. The thieves did not get Little Faith's jewels. Read Matthew 6:19–21 and John 10:28–29. What do these jewels represent in the life of a Christian?

8. Christian tells Hopeful that after the assault, Little Faith would not sell his jewels and was forced to beg to stay alive and complete his journey. This leads to a debate with Hopeful suggesting that Little Faith should have sold his jewels in order to pay his own way. Why is Christian astounded at Hopeful's comment and consider it lunacy? What is the difference between the money and the jewels?

9. Hopeful acknowledges his error but admits that he almost got angry with Christian's terse response. Christian encourages Hopeful not to take offense but to engage willingly in honest debate. We, too, will often have differences in our understanding of God's truth. When debating a theological issue, are you more concerned with winning your brother or winning the argument?

10. Hopeful wonders why Little Faith was not more courageous and did not put forth more effort to stand against the villains. What did Christian understand about Little Faith's trial that Hopeful did not? Read Galatians 6:3. Have you ever underestimated the power of sin in someone else's life or wondered why their situation is such a struggle?

11. The thieves took off when they thought they heard Great Grace coming. Read Hebrews 11:32–34. What type of Christian does Great Grace represent, and what are his limitations? Who are those "Great Grace" Christians in your life?

12. Christian compares the might of Apollyon to the sea serpent Leviathan, described in the book of Job, as a reminder of the overwhelming strength of the enemy and the tough road that is still in front of them. What warning does Christian give about desiring to meet our enemies, and what two things must we do if we do meet them? Read Ephesians 6:16, Psalm 23:4, and Exodus 33:15.

Session 11: Chapter 11

The Ensnarement of Flatterer

1. Throughout his journey, Christian has battled spiritual pride. His most recent battle was when he opted for an easier path into By-Path meadow, when the Way became too difficult, and was then led astray by Vain Confidence. Now he and Hopeful face the dilemma of two paths that seem to go in the same direction but do not. Like Christian, what sins that caused you to stumble in the past are still trying to trip you up today?

2. Why did Christian and Hopeful not recognize the stranger as the Flatterer? How were they lured into following him? Read 2 Corinthians 11:13–15. Who was the Flatterer later revealed to be?

3. According to Psalm 5:9 and Romans 16:18, how does a wise person learn to recognize and separate flattery from sincere compliments?

4. Soon Christian and Hopeful find themselves going in the opposite direction, subtly led away and then ensnared in a net before they know what is happening. According to Proverbs 29:5, what is the goal of the flatterer? In general, how do Christians get caught in the net of flattery?

5. They cry and repent of their sin of neglecting God's Word and of going astray then see an angel coming "with a whip made of small cords in his hand." What does the angel do to set them on the right path? Read Revelation 3:19, Proverbs 13:24, and Deuteronomy 25:2. What does the whip and whipping represent in the Christian life?

6. How did Christian and Hopeful respond to the angel's discipline? Read Psalm 141:5. How do you normally handle discipline or correction in your life?

7. Their song seems to be a confession of their sin for the benefit of helping others. Have you ever had the opportunity to share with others how the Lord disciplined you over a sin? Explain.

8. Ignorance is mentioned at the beginning as trailing behind, and we will see him again later in the story. Simply for conjecture, how do you think Ignorance avoided the snare that captured Christian and Hopeful?

The Laughter of Atheist

1. Christian and Hopeful become suspicious when they see a man, who does not appear threatening, walking "quietly and alone" toward them. Who is this man, and what do we learn about him?

2. When Christian tells Atheist that they are going to Mount Zion, how does he respond? An atheist is one who adamantly denies the existence of God and the truth of Scripture. What does the Bible mean in Psalm 53:1 when it says, "The fool says in his heart, 'There is no God'? Does this mean that atheists lack intelligence?

3. Atheist claims that he was once a serious pilgrim, just like them, and had carefully investigated the Christian life for over 20 years, finding it to be just a myth. Have you ever known someone who renounced the gospel after a period of years of professing it? What was their reasoning? How did their life change after rejecting God? How did they treat you?

4. How does Hopeful respond to Christian's question about whether they should believe Atheist? What does Paul mean in 2 Corinthians 5:7 when he says that we should walk by faith and not by sight? Read Proverbs 19:27. What instruction or teaching do you need to stop listening to before you are led astray?

5. Christian and Hopeful turn away from Atheist and resolve to press on, intent on reaching the Celestial City while believing what they know to be true and rejecting what they know to be a lie. Based on Atheist's response and Ephesians 2:12, what sort of future is in store for him?

Crossing the Enchanted Ground

1. As Christian and Hopeful near the end of their journey, they must travel through the Enchanted Ground. What danger does the Enchanted Ground represent? Scripture warns us of the dangers of spiritual slumber (Romans 13:11 and 1 Thessalonians 5:6), yet the enchanting air of this world lures unsuspecting Christians to sleep. How might this danger manifest itself in the life of a Christian?

2. Read Ecclesiastes 4:9–10 and Hebrews 3:13. How do Christian and Hopeful avoid danger and make it across the Enchanted Ground? Name someone in your life who has been a good accountability partner for you and explain why.

3. Their conversation begins with Christian asking Hopeful how he first became concerned with the condition of his soul. How does Hopeful describe his life prior to becoming a Christian? Describe your life prior to becoming a Christian.

4. Read Ephesians 5:3–7 and Romans 6:21. What was the turning point in Hopeful's life that led him to become concerned with his own spiritual state? What motivated you to become concerned with your spiritual state? What was it about another person's life that intrigued you to pursue faith?

5. Even with the great witness of Christian and Faithful, why didn't Hopeful immediately come to Christ? How was Hopeful eventually reminded of his sinfulness before God?

6. Hindered by his own thoughts and trying to find a way to ease his guilty conscience, Hopeful decides to mend his life by becoming a better person. Describe some of his efforts. What biblical truths did Hopeful come to understand from reading Ephesians 2:8–9 and Isaiah 64:6?

7. As Hopeful realizes the futility in trying to earn righteousness through his own efforts, he looks to Faithful for guidance. Read 2 Corinthians 5:21. What advice does Faithful give him, and what does he say about the righteousness of Christ alone being sufficient to save?

8. Hopeful wanted to believe Faithful, but he hesitated because he thought himself too great a sinner and did not believe God would be willing to save him. Faithful encouraged him to go and find out for himself since he was invited to do so. Why might people today believe God would be unwilling to save them? In Matthew 11:28–30, who is Jesus's inviting to come, and what burden is he talking about?

9 Faithful encouraged Hopeful to take God at His Word and go to Him in repentance and faith. According to Psalm 95:6 and Jeremiah 29:12–13, how did Faithful instruct Hopeful to approach God?

10. Because of his fears, doubts, and guilt of past sins, Hopeful struggled coming to Christ and prayed many times before he truly laid hold of Christ in the gospel. This is similar to Christian knocking multiple times at the Wicket Gate before he was allowed in. Today's evangelism presents a quicker and easier portrayal of Christian conversion, whereas Bunyan describes it more as a period of intense conflict. How would you describe your conversion?

11. At the point of Hopeful's conversion, he was flooded with the awareness of the enormity of his sin while still struggling with the thought that he was too bad to be saved. This awareness came by searching the Scriptures to find answers to the questions that were concerning him. What did Hopeful come to understand about belief?

12. When Hopeful understood the truth of God's Word concerning salvation in Christ, how did it change his worldview? How has your worldview changed as you have matured as a Christian?

Ignorance Follows His Heart

1. Like Christian and Hopeful, Ignorance has continued walking along the Way but appears to regard the journey more casually. What kinds of danger might one expect from a casual approach to the Christian life?

2. When asked about his relationship with God, Ignorance says that he fills his mind with "good thoughts" that comfort him. Using the following verses, how does Christian demonstrate that "good thoughts" are insufficient for a saving faith?

A) Thinking about God and heaven (James 2:19) –

B) Desiring God and heaven (Proverbs 13:4) –

C) Trusting in his own heart (Proverbs 28:26 and Jeremiah 17:9–10) –

3. Ignorance wrongly assumes his heart to be good and in agreement with his life. What does Christian tell him the only true measure of the heart is? Popular opinion says to follow your heart. Why is that bad advice for a Christian?

4. Using Romans 3:10–12, Genesis 6:5, and Genesis 8:21, how does Christian instruct Ignorance as to the difference between a believer and nonbeliever's thoughts about their hearts?

5. Ignorance refuses to believe the truth that his heart is bad, which keeps him from understanding and receiving the righteousness of Christ. How would you help someone who truly believes they have a good heart, are leading a good life, and therefore are on the right path to heaven?

6. Ignorance's thoughts about God are shaped by his experience and imagination rather than what the Word says about Him. How have your experiences and imagination shaped your thoughts about God?

7. Ignorance is not rebellious or intentionally deceptive. Rather, he's sincere in what he believes and earnest in his conversation with Christian. His problem is that he has made himself (or his heart and feelings) the standard for what he believes rather than the truth of God's Word. In what areas in your life do you find it easier to listen to your heart rather than be confronted with the truth found in God's Word?

8. Ignorance rightly believes that Christ died on the cross for sinners, but he thinks that his justification rests in his own obedience to God's law. Read Galatians 2:15–16. What does Christian rightly conclude about Ignorance's faith?

9. Ignorance wrongly assumes that free grace from God would encourage sinners to continue in their sin. What is Paul's response to the rhetorical question in Romans 6:1–2 as to whether we should continue in sin in order to experience more of His grace?

10. Ignorance believes his faith is as good as Hopeful's and does not see any need to have God "reveal" Himself to him and open his heart. What do the following verses say about God's sovereignty in revealing Himself to us? What is our responsibility to God's calling?

2 Corinthians 4:6 –

John 6:44 –

Ephesians 1:17–19 –

Ephesians 4:17–18 –

The Backsliding of Temporary

1. As Ignorance falls behind once again, the two pilgrims begin to feel sorry for him. What do Christian and Hopeful identify as the root cause for Ignorance's failure to grasp the seriousness of sin?

2. How does Christian say that you can identify true godly fear? What do the following verses claim that fear of the Lord leads to?

Psalm 111:10 –

Matthew 10:28 –

Psalm 128:1 –

Proverbs 14:26 (NKJV) –

3. How does Christian explain the nonbeliever's attempt to suppress fear and conviction? Why do you think many in our day have lost a fear of the Lord or believe that godly fear is weakness?

4. Christian remembers a former pilgrim named Temporary. How might Temporary's background provide insight into his spiritual condition, and what sort of pilgrim might he represent?

5. What is your definition of the term "backsliding"? How does Bunyan define the term? Can you point to a time in your life when you would have considered yourself backslidden?

6. Although the word "backslide" is not in the Bible, the phrase "fall away" is. It has two different meanings. In one, the person is saved but experiences a temporary "crisis of faith," and in the other, the person is not saved and only temporarily behaving as if they were. Read the following verses, and identify which definition applies.

Mark 14:27 –

Galatians 6:1 –

Hebrews 6:4–6 –

Luke 8:13 –

7. List the four reasons that Hopeful suggests as to why people like Temporary backslide. Why do you think people backslide today?

8. Christian offers nine reasons that follow the progression of sin for a backslider. Put them in order below.

_____ They begin to rationalize their sin and do it openly.

_____ They avoid godly friends.

_____ They surround themselves with unbelievers.

_____ They stop thinking about anything that reminds them of God.

_____ They start finding faults in other believers.

_____ They find their hearts hardened and worse off than before.

_____ They stop attending church.

_____ They give in to immoral and ungodly conversations.

_____ They neglect personal Christian responsibilities.

Session 12: Chapter 12
The Country of Beulah

1. After a long and wearisome journey through the Enchanted Ground, the pilgrims arrive in the country of Beulah, where they are within sight of the Celestial City. In Isaiah 62:1–12, the Hebrew word Beulah means married and speaks of a time when God will be reunited with his bride, Israel, after a long exile. Considering the definition and Scripture text, what period of the Christian life do you think Bunyan is suggesting this represents?

2. Using the story passage as well as Isaiah 62:1–12 and Song of Songs 2:10–12, describe the land of Beulah.

3. Beulah is a land where doubt and despair no longer trouble seasoned pilgrims like Christian and Hopeful. Their days are drawing to an end, and the world no longer enthralls them as they begin to think solely of eternity. What does it mean in Ecclesiastes 3:11 that we have eternity in our hearts?

4. Christian and Hopeful are overwhelmed by the sight of the glory of the Celestial City and become homesick, longing to be with Christ. How does Paul express his longing to be with Christ in Philippians 1:21–23? What does it mean to live is Christ? What is the gain of death for a Christian?

5. Christian and Hopeful are at that stage in the journey where their greatest desire is to be with Christ. It's much easier to say, "To live is Christ," than to say, "To die is gain." Do you really feel that death is a gain and not some horrible experience you have to face? How might your thoughts about death be different than that of a nonbeliever?

The River of Death

1. As Christian and Hopeful near the end of their journey and are within sight of the Celestial City, they are accompanied by angels who inform them that they must cross a deep and foreboding river to reach the gate of the City. Read 1 Corinthians 15:26. What does the river barrier represent in the Christian life?

2. The pilgrims ask if there's any other way to the gate. They are told there is, but Scripture speaks of only two people whom God took to heaven without them dying: Enoch and Elijah. Describe their stories in Genesis 5:23–24, Hebrews 11:5, and 2 Kings 2:11.

3. The pilgrims soon realize that death is unavoidable. When you think of your own impending death, what thoughts and feelings come to mind? How can you prepare yourself mentally, spiritually, and emotionally for it?

4. What did the angels mean when they said that the pilgrims would find the river of death "deeper or shallower according to their trust in the King of this place"?

5. Read Psalm 42:7 and 69:1–2 and describe Christian's response to the river of death upon entering it.

6. Read Psalm 73:2–5 and describe Hopeful's response to the river of death upon entering it.

7. Hopeful encourages Christian to remember the promises of God. What promises of God does Scripture offer regarding death in the following passages?

Philippians 1:21–23 –

2 Timothy 4:6–8 –

Isaiah 43:2 –

Psalm 23:4 –

Hebrews 13:5–6 –

8. Share an experience of being with someone who was close to death. What feelings did they share with you? Were they confident in their faith, or did they seem more distressed? How did their death affect you?

A Heavenly Welcome

1. As Christian and Hopeful are ushered by angels to the Celestial City, they shed their mortal bodies and put on immortality. Read 2 Corinthians 5:1–5. In what sense are our bodies like tents? If we were to truly look forward to our "house not made with hands," how would it affect our daily lives here?

2. Although it's impossible to fully grasp and describe the splendor of heaven, Bunyan does not merely speculate but instead points us to Scripture. Summarize in a few words how heaven is described in each Scripture passage below.

Hebrews 12:22–24 –

Revelation 2:7 –

Revelation 3:4 –

Revelation 21:4 –

Revelation 22:3–4 –

Isaiah 57:1–2 –

Matthew 8:11 –

Galatians 6:7–8 –

1 Corinthians 15:51–52 –

1 Corinthians 6:2–3 –

1 Thessalonians 4:13–18 –

Revelation 19:6–9 –

3. At the gate, each pilgrim is asked to present their certificate to gain entrance into the City. Christian received his certificate from the angel at the cross and was told that he must provide it at the Celestial Gate. Referring to Chapter 3, what does the certificate represent?

4. As Christian and Hopeful enter into glory, Bunyan concludes his account by wishing he could be with them. What is it about heaven that you look forward to the most?

5. Bunyan turns to look back, and he sees Ignorance crossing over the river with ease in a boat steered by Vain-Hope then arriving at the gate with no one to greet him. Read Luke 13:24–26. What assumption did Ignorance make as he stood knocking at the gate? Looking back at his life, why would he assume this?

6. When Ignorance is asked for his certificate, he is speechless. Read Matthew 22:11–14. Who does the man without the wedding clothes represent? Why is this considered such a serious offense?

7. Read Matthew 7:21–23. Why do you think Bunyan chose to conclude his story with this sober warning?

8. Bunyan opens *The Pilgrim's Progress* by describing his book as a dream and closes it in the same fashion. What is it about his "dream" that has impacted you the most?

Leave a Review

Thank you again for doing this Bible study! I hope and pray that in some way, it encouraged you (and your group) to grow closer to Christ.

If you enjoyed this study, I would appreciate your leaving an honest review for the book and study on Amazon! Your review will help others know if this study is right for them and their small group.

It's easy and will only take a minute. Just search for "The Pilgrim's Progress Study Guide, Alan Vermilye" on Amazon. Click on the product in the search results, and then click on reviews.

I would also love to hear from you! Drop me a note by visiting me at www.BrownChairBooks.com and clicking on "Contact."

Thank you and God bless!

Alan

Other Studies from Brown Chair Books

On the following pages, you'll find information from some of our other Bible studies.

www.BrownChairBooks.com

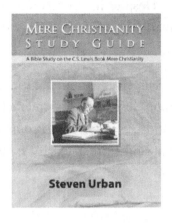

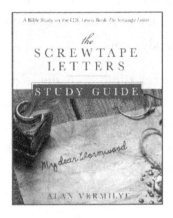

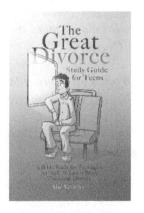

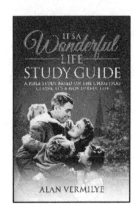

MERE CHRISTIANITY STUDY GUIDE

A Bible Study on the C.S. Lewis Book *Mere Christianity*

By Steven Urban

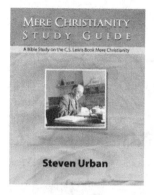

Mere Christianity Study Guide takes participants through a study of C.S. Lewis's classic, *Mere Christianity*. Despite its recognition as a "classic," there is surprisingly little available today in terms of a serious study course.

This 12-week Bible study digs deep into each chapter and, in turn, into Lewis's thoughts. Perfect for small group sessions, this interactive workbook includes daily, individual study as well as a complete appendix and commentary to supplement and further clarify certain topics. Multiple-week format options are also included.

What others are saying:

This study guide is more than just a guide to C.S Lewis's Mere Christianity*; it is a guide to Christianity itself.* – Crystal

Wow! What a lot of insight and food for thought! Perfect supplement to Mere Christianity. *I think Mr. Lewis himself would approve.* – Laurie

Our group is in the middle of studying Mere Christianity, *and I have found this guide to be invaluable.* – Angela

This is a very useful and comprehensive guide to Mere Christianity. – John

Preview a chapter sample and read reviews at Amazon!

THE SCREWTAPE LETTERS STUDY GUIDE
A Bible Study on the C.S. Lewis Book *The Screwtape Letters*
By Alan Vermilye

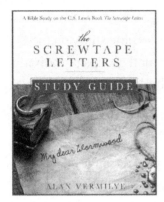

The Screwtape Letters Study Guide takes participants through a study of C.S. Lewis's classic, *The Screwtape Letters*.

This Bible study digs deep into each letter from Screwtape, an undersecretary in the lowerarchy of hell, to his incompetent nephew, Wormwood, a junior devil. Perfect for small group sessions, this interactive workbook includes daily, individual study with a complete answer guide available online.

Designed as a 12-week study, multiple-week format options are also included.

What others are saying:

This book and study create a positive reinforcement on fighting that spiritual battle in life. Great read, great study guide! – Lester

This study guide was a wonderful way for our group to work through The Screwtape Letters*!* – Becky

Use this Study Guide for a fresh "seeing" of The Screwtape Letters*!* – William

This is an essential companion if you are reading The Screwtape Letters *as a small group.* – J.T.

Preview a chapter sample and read reviews at Amazon!

THE GREAT DIVORCE STUDY GUIDE

A Bible Study on the C.S. Lewis Book *The Great Divorce*

By Alan Vermilye

The Great Divorce Study Guide is an eight-week Bible study on the C.S. Lewis classic, *The Great Divorce*. Perfect for small groups or individual study, each weekly study session applies a biblical framework to the concepts found in each chapter of the book. Although intriguing and entertaining, much of Lewis's writings can be difficult to grasp.

The Great Divorce Study Guide will guide you through each one of Lewis's masterful metaphors to a better understanding of the key concepts of the book, the supporting Bible passages, and the relevance to our world today. Each study question is ideal for group discussion, and answers to each question are available online.

What others are saying:

To my knowledge, there have not been many study guides for either of these, so to see this new one on The Great Divorce *(both electronic and print) is a welcome sight!* – Richard

I recommend The Great Divorce Study Guide *to anyone or any group wishing to delve more deeply into the question, why would anyone choose hell over heaven!* – Ruth

The questions were thought-provoking, and I very much liked how everything was evaluated by scripture. Would definitely recommend! – Justin

Preview a chapter sample and read reviews at Amazon!

THE PROBLEM OF PAIN STUDY GUIDE
A Bible Study on the C.S. Lewis Book *The Problem of Pain*
By Alan Vermilye

Why must humanity suffer? Why doesn't God alleviate our pain, even some?

In his book, *The Problem of Pain*, C.S. Lewis's philosophical approach to why we experience pain can be confusing at times. *The Problem of Pain Study Guide* breaks down each chapter into easy-to-understand questions and commentary to help you find meaning and hope amid the pain.

The Problem of Pain Study Guide expands upon Lewis's elegant and thoughtful work, where he seeks to understand how a loving, good, and powerful God can possibly coexist with the pain and suffering that is so pervasive in the world and in our lives. As Christ-followers, we might expect the world to be just, fair, and less painful, but it is not. This is the problem of pain.

What others are saying:

Many thanks for lending me a helping hand with one of the greatest thinkers of all time! – Adrienne

The questions posed range from very straightforward (to help the reader grasp main concepts) to more probing (to facilitate personal application), while perhaps the greatest benefit they supply is their tie-in of coordinating scriptures that may not always be apparent to the reader. – Sphinn

The questions are thought-provoking and biblically based! – Jen

Preview a chapter sample and read reviews at Amazon!

A CHRISTMAS CAROL STUDY GUIDE
Book and Bible Study Based on *A Christmas Carol*
By Alan Vermilye

A Christmas Carol Book and Bible Study Guide includes the entire book of this Dickens classic as well as Bible study discussion questions for each chapter, Scripture references, and related commentary.

Detailed character sketches and an easy-to-read book summary provide deep insights into each character while examining the book's themes of greed, isolation, guilt, blame, compassion, generosity, transformation, forgiveness, and, finally, redemption. To help with those more difficult discussion questions, a complete answer guide is available for free online.

What others are saying:

The study is perfect for this time of the year, turning our focus to the reason for the season–Jesus–and the gift of redemption we have through him. – Connie

I used this for an adult Sunday School class. We all loved it! – John

This study is wonderful! – Lori

I found this a refreshing look at the Bible through the eyes of Ebenezer Scrooge's life. – Lynelle

Preview a chapter sample and read reviews at Amazon!

IT'S A WONDERFUL STUDY GUIDE
A Bible Study Based on the Christmas Classic *It's a   Wonderful Life*
By Alan Vermilye

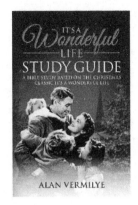

It's a Wonderful Life is one of the most popular and heartwarming films ever made. It's near universal appeal and association with Christmas has provided a rich story of redemption that has inspired generations for decades.

It's a Wonderful Life Study Guide examines this beloved holiday classic and reminds us how easily we can become distracted from what is truly meaningful in life. This five-week Bible study experience comes complete with discussion questions for each session, Scripture references, detailed character sketches, a movie summary, and related commentary. In addition, a complete answer guide and video segments for each session are available for free online.

What others are saying:

Thank you, Alan for, the unforgettable experience. Your book has prompted me to see and learn much more than merely enjoying the film, It's a Wonderful Life. – Er Jwee

The questions got us all thinking, and the answers provided were insightful and encouraging. I would definitely encourage Home Groups to study this! – Jill

It's a Wonderful Life Study Guide *by Alan Vermilye is intelligent, innovative, interesting, involving, insightful, and inspirational.* – Paul

Preview a chapter sample and read reviews at Amazon!